Overachiever's Diary

Louis Tharp
with Laurie J. Ferguson, Ph.D.

Total Immersion, Inc.
New Paltz, New York

Overachiever's Diary

http://www.overachieversdiary.com

Published in the United States by Total Immersion, Inc.

This book is not an official publication
of the U.S. Military Academy.

Tharp, Louis C. (Louis Clay), 1951–
Ferguson, Laurie J., Ph.D., 1955–

ISBN 978-1-931009-12-6

Text and cover design: Richard Tjoa
Photo Editor, Proofreader: Brett Wiggins
Cover photo by Scott Strine, West Point '88. Proudly capturing
events building accountability and character at
http://www.jump71.com

First Edition: October 2007

Contents

Introduction

Terry Laughlin, founder
Total Immersion Swimming
http://www.totalimmersion.net

I met Lou Tharp in 1998 when he attended a TI Weekend Workshop in New Paltz as a swimmer whose motivation to learn was as keen as his skills were raw. Because his curiosity about and passion for swimming was a match for mine, we became fast friends.

I knew that Lou had an unusually demanding job as the founder of a health promotion company, that evidently required long hours (whether I

Terry Laughlin

email Lou before 5:00 A.M. or after 10:00 P.M., I regularly receive an immediate reply) and considerable travel, often international. Thus I couldn't help notice how readily he would interrupt work to travel 30 to 45 minutes to Manhattan or West Point from his Nyack home and office to swim—or spend an hour on the phone with me talking swimming in the middle of his workday (justifiable as "work related" for me but not him). His efforts paid off in steady improvement and a growing collection of Masters medals.

Lou's interest soon evolved from improving his own swimming to helping others, prompting him to steal more time from work to gain experience as an unpaid assistant coach at TI workshops or camps. Swimming had become a consuming passion for the sake of which he endured the inconvenience of having to pay the bills with non-swimming activities. Seeing in Lou a passion unmatched by many who do pay the bills by coaching swimming I suggested that he was really meant to coach swimming and speculated on when that would happen.

So it was no surprise when, in 2005, Lou told me he'd begun helping the West Point Triathlon Club as a volunteer swim coach. Soon after, emails from Lou began to arrive in my inbox once or twice a week—copies of messages he composed to announce the day's practice to team members. That's unusual in itself. Most coaches just call out the set from the deck. The more ambitious among them write sets on a whiteboard. Lou—an unpaid assistant—was making sure his athletes could come to each session with the kind of mental preparation that was his custom. But he didn't just detail the day's sets and reps. Each message examined a fundamental aspect of how to develop as a swimmer and explained how that day's practice related to it. And there was more. With a gifted teacher's knack for enriching a lesson by placing it in a broader context, Lou would usually relate the swimming concept to other aspects of triathlon or life at the Academy. And finally, every message was an engrossing read.

I'd never seen anything like these before. Not just the exceptional nature of thoroughly explaining the effects and benefits of each practice, but how the series cumulatively constituted a seminar on how swimming really works. As Lou's message archive grew I realized that a collection of a full season's worth of "diary entries" would be uniquely enlightening to improvement-minded swimmers, especially those who are self-coached, as well as a complete chronicle of a season of triathlon-swim-training in which every training set had a clearly defined purpose.

So I suggested to Lou that we publish an annotated collection of a full season of his messages in book form. *Overachiever's Diary* is the result. This surprising book, from an "unknown" coach and swimmer will help you look at swimming through new eyes—and learn something new—every time you visit the pool. It's a fresh, funny and creative look at swimming that is simple to understand and, best of all (as demonstrated by the progress shown by the West Point triathletes), will bring proven results. Spend a season with the *Overachiever's Diary* and you'll realize the pleasure in swimming comes as much from learning as from winning.

About Me

Louis Tharp

I have a swimmer's body, but when I began swimming at age 45, I had a sitter's belly.

Getting close to 300 pounds and seeing the first signs of what happens to your health when you sit around with that much weight, I stopped working 80 hours a week at a job I didn't like and put together what was jokingly referred to as Team Tharp—a nutritionist, a psychologist, a chiropractor, a couple of alternative medicine MDs, a conservative traditional medicine MD, a trainer of course, a yoga instructor, and a swim coach.

Actually, the swim coach part wasn't as simple picking up the phone. The nicest way to describe a lot of swim coaches was that they were stuck somewhere in the '70s. Although at the time I couldn't identify the decade, I knew the information I was getting was wrong. Pull buoys made no sense to me, kick boards even less. Paddles and fins were a good example of cognitive dissonance. I began slogging through practices hoping to get faster by doing the same thing I did the day before.

I spent the first six months flailing in the water and complaining until I found Total Immersion and took a weekend workshop. Although I loved the water, swimming was not intuitive. TI made it second nature. I asked Terry Laughlin, founder of TI, if he would coach me and he declined, so we started an email correspondence and sometimes swam together. Afterwards I'd email what we discussed and what I learned—not the practice—and he'd reply. He coined the term "Team Tharp." One day when I thought I was swimming particularly well, but couldn't do a drill, he said that since I'd been swimming for about two years, I was roughly at the level of a nine-year-old. Perspective is his strength, and he's agreed to publish the book and write the introduction. I call him my coach.

Life went on. I competed and medaled at World Masters, at many other international, local and regional age-group meets, and was fortunate enough to train at the U.S. Olympic Training Center in Colorado Springs. I lost nearly 80 pounds, got as buff as I could, became a swim camp junkie where I met Bill Boomer, Richard Quick and Skip Kenney at Stanford, and took on the identity of an athlete for the first time in my life.

Growing up gay in the '60s and '70s meant not playing sports even if you had a swimmer's body. Being gay then was a mental defect and a crime in the United States—jocks weren't gay. A lot has changed—we're no longer crazy criminals. But a lot hasn't. I think about what kind of swimmer I'd be today if I had felt more comfortable participating in swimming in high school and college. Having learned under the best coaches of the day, I'd have gotten burned out after 10,000 yard practices and have all the bad habits of the guys in my age group I regularly beat.

I swam regularly at West Point—usually by myself. One day a cadet was swimming in the lane next me and his stroke was so bad I stopped him and said, in the nicest way possible, that his technique was so awful I couldn't focus on my own practice.

We spent the next 30 minutes working together. He was like a sponge and his improvement was dramatic. He wanted to get better and could hardly have gotten worse. The next day there were two cadets and the following week they invited me to their tri team swim practice.

During the '07 season we were in Galveston at a pre-collegiate nationals event, and, as usual, the local West Point parents club got together and hosted the team. As I was walking through the buffet line at the beach-front home, a very Texas mother with a very Texas voice and a big Texas-shaped name tag asked where I had coached before, and I realized that I was coaching a Division I school with no resume. And we were successful. Preparation met opportunity—the strength of the existing coaching staff, the positive nurturing structure of the U.S. Military Academy, and the desire of everyone on the team to excel combined to produce results that took five people to Age Group Nationals and came home with gold, a team fifth in collegiate nationals, and invitations to the upcoming Sprint Nationals in Hamburg.

After 35 years as a journalist, marketer and author, I became a social entrepreneur at the urging of an intern, Seth Ginsberg, who was diagnosed with arthritis at 13. Today we run TGI Healthworks which we co-founded, and in 2006, started the Global Healthy Living Foundation—an operating charity. Both organizations work to improve the quality of life for people with chronic disease worldwide. A third member of our team, Laurie Ferguson, Ph.D., is a contributor to this book. Her thoughts appear in the motivation section. As a writer and a powerful motivational speaker, Laurie and I speak to corporate, fraternal and civic groups about doing what you want with your life and contributing to the world through individual actions. The final person who contributed to this book should be called my husband, but we're currently stuck with the interim inarticulate "domestic partner in a civil union" label. Jim Bumgardner and I have been together 24 years and although his words are not on these pages, his heart is.

About
Laurie J. Ferguson, Ph.D.

Laurie Ferguson and I have known each other for more than 15 years. During that time she's been my minister and then my business associate. She is a powerful motivational speaker, and an overachiever in her own right.

Laurie J. Ferguson, Ph.D.

She graduated *cum laude* with high honors from Smith College in 1977, received her Masters of Divinity from Princeton Theological Seminary in 1980, and received her Ph.D. in Psychology from the Derner Institute at Adelphi University in 2004, where her dissertation topic was "Coaching for Hardiness: A Study of Clergywomen and Stress."

Laurie and I speak to corporate, civic, sports, high school, university, and fraternal groups about swimming, staying focused on goals, and motivation.

It's about emails

Overachiever's Diary is a compilation of emails that I wrote to cadets on the tri team. So while you're reading this book, put yourself in an email frame of mind. I've also left much of the contact intact so you can get the sense of being there. Sometimes before chapters I'll give a little back story, but usually you'll just get thrown into the email as if you were part of the team.

I've split the book into three sections: Mechanics, Math, and Motivation—and it's roughly in chronological order. When I first came to West Point in the '05–'06 school year, we worked for a season on mechanics. The first half of '06–'07 was mechanics, too. Then we went into the math part of getting better in the water. I wanted a way that the cadets, as well as the coaches, could objectively see improvement over time.

The only way to do this was to quantify movement in the water. Using height (taller people have a natural advantage in the water), distance per stroke, and stroke rate algorithm, Terry Laughlin and I came up with a way to measure progress as well as future goals. Using this assessment tool, the cadets were able to chart their progress quantitatively, regardless of their temporary training state—and usually that was close to physical exhaustion.

The team was encouraged to answer the emails—and many did. As you can imagine, training was arduous and was combined with a heavy course load, as well as physical and mental military training—so the emails back to me were often personal—reflecting the hopes, failures, dreams, goals and successes of the cadets. I've reprinted a few in the book, but not very many. Our team was a place where people were encouraged to try and fail—and try again. Their privacy is paramount if we are going to keep this an open atmosphere of trust and confidence.

It's also about photos

There are many photos in this book. None were taken by a professional photographer. Cadets and their family donated these pictures. Cadet Joe Imbriaco's mother, Lynn; Cadet Nick Vandam's brother, Patrick; Cadet Mike Noel's mother, Penny; Cadet Ashley Morgan's mother, Donna; and Cadets Andy Cahoy, Nick Dason, Erica Triebenbach, Nick Vandam, Bryan Lagasse, John Leatherman, Emily Sfeir and a few others who I couldn't identify from the pictures, donated their photos. They have my thanks. As much as I'd like to think the writing is good enough to keep you interested, the photos tell a story by themselves.

And it's about keeping the Tri Team strong

I couldn't have written this book without the support and cooperation of the Army Tri Team and its coaching staff. When you are able to get a glimpse of the West Point tradition and see the dedication of these student soldiers, as I have, you respect their commitment to themselves, to West Point, and to their country. I think service academies should be exempt from military budget cutters.

You quickly understand that service academies are the strongest force for peace in the world because the teachers understand war. It's not surprising that I also think the Army Triathlon team is vital to the continuing development of mentally and physically strong soldiers. So when we first discussed writing a book about Army Tri, I was committed to giving a share of the proceeds of the book back to the team to help ensure its continuation.

And it's about
Total Immersion

Total Immersion (http://www.totalimmersion.net) is the publisher of this book, and its contents reflect my interpretation of TI philosophy and technique. I'm an unabashed disciple of Total Immersion principles. Terry Laughlin noted when he read the pre-publication copy of the book that there were sections that contained his words and thoughts almost exactly. I took that as a complement, even though I wasn't aware that I had done that. Terry helped me get the job at West Point and encouraged me to put my emails into this book.

His guidance and the foundation that his TI structure provides is invaluable. I believe you have two substantive choices in swimming, you can get better with TI or you can beat yourself up mentally and physically with other teaching and training methods. I choose to get better, and TI provides the inspiration and solid thinking that I can incorporate into my own drive.

When I coach, I try to adhere to the TI thought process of continually examining everything I do, trying to stay open to new ideas, reexamining old ideas that I don't respect, listening to the swimmers, and regular quantitative measuring in order to track progress, or lack thereof.

If this stuff didn't work, I wouldn't be coaching at West Point. I wasn't hired because of my long history of success. I'm not tenured. I'm not a mover or a shaker in the swimming world. I'm a person who was fortunate enough to have the chance to prove what I thought the tri team could do in the water. I was given tremendous latitude within an organization that many people think isn't capable of providing it. Those people are wrong.

And it's about
the officers in charge

There is a unique dynamic that may exist with other club teams at West Point, but I've only had the opportunity to witness it with the tri team. When a group of students wants to achieve, and the officers in charge not only agree with them—but understand how to help them do it—there is very little that gets in the way of success.

Like other club teams, the triathlon team does not possess overly abundant resources, has to be thrifty, and has many systemic obstacles to success. Cadet training and academic schedules squeeze tri training into a very small module. Equipment isn't always first rate; pool time can be hard to schedule.

The head coach, Colonel Pat Sullivan, and the officer in charge, Lt. Colonel Ralph Vargas, as well as Donna Vargas, the physical therapist and trainer—came to their jobs with seriousness, open minds, a high sense of resourcefulness, and extensive, current triathlon résumés. The atmosphere they created allowed the cadets to have faith in their training and in themselves. It gave everyone the ability to plan for the unexpected and react in productive ways. It gave me, with virtually no provenance, the tools to prove what I knew would work in the water. Before I could do this, there had to be a team—and I got a great one because of the smart, hard work of the officers in charge.

Don't Get Frustrated

This book is written in Army Tri team language. It's only part of the training experience. When you find a phrase that doesn't make sense, or a concept I don't sufficiently explain, go to http://www.totalimmersion.net and then to the *Overachiever's Diary* discussion board and let me know what you need to know. I read the boards regularly and will further explain anything I was remiss in covering completely in this book.

To the Army Tri Cadets who came to practice ready to learn.

*You enjoyed success and endured frustration
on the way to becoming champions.*

You were never complacent.

Section 1: Mechanics

Hello, Everyone

Wednesday, 8 February

I typically begin my emails with "Hello Everyone," so it seemed like a good way to start the first chapter. There was the usual pressure to get good quickly, self-imposed pressure by the team, so I adopted a system of fundamentals until they became frustrating. We'd then move into more demanding practice sets and stroke would fall apart. This allowed the team to understand the need for fundamentals. Once this concept was clear, we began "focus 50s," where the team would perform dynamic drills for 50 yards and then get 10 seconds of mental focus and a new drill from me for the next 50. By watching the team's stroke mechanics and incorporating drills that improved stroke, we were able to see immediate positive results without spending a lot of time talking about what they were doing wrong. I don't like to tell cadets what they are doing wrong. It's my job to identify the problem, not verbalize it, and to ask them to try something new that fixes it—without discussing the problem. They see that modifying their stroke can produce immediate improve-

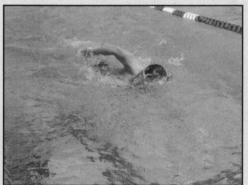

ments, and that's what's important—not what they were doing wrong. It is also important for cadets to understand why they are doing drills. It is critical to keep the brain connected to the body so both can improve.

At Tuesday night's practice you counted strokes. Why

- Consistent swimming is measured in the pool by knowing the number of strokes you take for each 25 yard segment measured against time.

- The more strokes you take, the more energy you burn in the first stage of a triathlon—energy that won't be available for biking or running.

- Understanding your maximum cruising speed at a minimum stroke count puts you in control of your glycogen usage—saving energy for biking and running.

- When you want to learn to swim faster in the pool, you increase stroke count—to a point. By counting strokes against time you understand the point at which increasing your stroke count does not increase speed, and ultimately will decrease your speed. This is wasted energy.

your speed. This is wasted energy.

You want to find the optimum stroke count for your race pace that allows you to swim at your peak. Your peak is defined as the fastest you can swim with a low heart rate, burning the least amount of glycogen.

This is why you count strokes.

Joe Imbriaco '07

Erin King '08

Maintain Speed, Reduce Strokes

Wednesday, 1 March

Tuesday night we looked at stroke count from a speed perspective. The objective was to take fewer strokes but maintain speed.

Why?

At the National Training Center, Clermont, Fla. for Spring Break '07

- You want to take fewer strokes so you use less energy and keep your heart rate down—but maintain the speed you had with more strokes and a high heart rate.

This is not as difficult as it might sound. Several people replicated their 50-yard pace with fewer strokes, and others were only two-three seconds slower in the 50. A lot of people are still working out the mental/physical/neuromuscular combination necessary to go fast efficiently, proving once again that we're glad you're smart, because swimming is for smart people.

How do you take fewer strokes and keep the same speed?

Swim Coach Louis Tharp

- Reduce drag. Just as good is the enemy of great[1], resistance is the enemy of power. The faster you go, the more resistance you encounter. So it is critical to eliminate as much drag as possible, and, at the same time, ensure power from the core is transferred to to you arms for propulsion. This is mental as well as physical.

- Reduce drag. The physical part is reducing drag by being streamlined and quiet in the water. Visualize the body as a cylinder that cuts through the water with as little disturbance as possible.

- Apply power. Power comes from your core, not from your arms and legs. When you are able to invoke a kinetic chain of energy that starts as you rotate your hips, goes to your abs, then lats then traps and delts, you are able to use your arms as power delivery systems, not power generators. Think of a pitcher chest-high in sand. Now ask the pitcher to throw a fast ball. Because the pitcher has to rely on the strength of arms only, the ball has little distance, and even less speed. However, when the pitcher is able to stand on the mound and invoke the kinetic chain that starts at the feet and torques through the body, the result is an efficient fast ball. Using only your arms to swim is like pitching in sand up to your chest.

Taking maximum advantage of your kinetic chain is critical to a lower heart rate and stroke count in combination with a faster pace.

Next week:

- Watch Tony's[2] elbows use gravity to decrease his stroke count and increase his speed.

- Experience the speed and efficiency of quiet swimming.

1. Jim Collins, *Good To Great: Why Some Companies Make the Leap... And Others Don't*, 2001 Harper Collins

2. Cadet Anthony Snipes '06

Andy Cahoy '10

Increase Speed, Control Strokes

Tuesday, 7 March

Tonight's main set allowed everyone to have the opportunity to increase speed while controlling stroke count—and map this increase against heart rate. Why?

As you increase speed, heart rate will go up. However, increasing your stroke count dramatically—what many swimmers do to increase speed—increases heart rate just as dramatically. The objective tonight was to swim at higher speeds efficiently so that stroke count stayed under control. The best way to do this is to swim with as little turbulence and resistance as possible. As resistance is reduced, speed increases and stroke count remains constant.

> "Set a goal of *Swimming Better Than You Ever Have in Your Life* in every practice."
>
> Terry Laughlin, founder
> Total Immersion Swimming

TI* Multisport Director Greg Sautner

Review from the white board:

Practice Makes Permanent. Swim with your best possible technique all the time.

Keep a low heart rate by swimming efficiently.

Keep stroke count consistent. (It will go up by one or two as you speed up, but if it jumps three or more, that's a signal that your swimming has become inefficient.

Practice Quiet Swimming. Silent swimmers go faster with less effort.

*Total Immersion

Joe Imbriaco '07, Dave Tyson '07

Transition practice.
Peter Bauleke '10,
Ryan Peacock '09

Peter Bauleke '10

Race Preparation

Wednesday, 22 March

> *Training periods and race schedules aren't always arranged in the order we'd like. Untapered race preparation is very different from a typical lead-up to a race—and when a team isn't stroke-ready, it's more different still. Asking a team to go hard for the first 200 meters of a tri swim if they aren't mechanically or psychologically prepared is a recipe for disaster in the second 200 meters. This email took these realities into consideration.*

Strategy: Warm-up

Why: If you swim without warm-up, you will go into an anaerobic state immediately. Oxygen has to get to your muscles before you start to swim for aerobic state swimming. Get your heart rate to 130 for five minutes minimum through jogging, other aerobics, then rehearse focal points and practice sighting for another five to 10 minutes in the water.

Joe Imbriaco '07, Andy Cahoy '10

Strategy: Swim the first 100 meters at a pace 50 percent slower than you think you should be swimming.

Why: You're excited. Slow down. How do you know when you've swum 100 meters? Count your strokes—20 strokes per 25 yards is about 100 strokes for 100 meters.

Strategy: Sight no more often than every 20 strokes.

Why: Sighting requires energy that isn't swimming. You lift your head and your hips drop, which increases resistance. You have to re-balance and this takes time and more energy. Also, don't look for buoys every time you sight. See where the pack is going. Stay with the pack. Look for buoys when you are nearly on top of them.

Strategy: Think about focal points while swimming.

Why: Keeps you aware of your efficiency. A menu of possible focal points:

- Head in-line with spine.

- Use your hand to lengthen your bodyline.

- Patient catch. Take time to firmly anchor hand before each stroke.

- Relaxed kicking. Your kick should be passive and almost unconscious.

- Silent swimming. Be the "quiet center" of whatever pack you're in.

- Zen swimming. Never chase the swimmers ahead of you. Instead, allow them to come back to you as the race progresses. Absorb the energy of the group. Be kind to your body. If you get hurt, allow your body to continue to do the job you've trained it for without wasting energy getting angry.

Swim coach Louis Tharp and Nick Vandam '09

Strategy: Existential swimming (making rational decisions despite irrational

*Joe Imbriaco '07, Bryan Lagasse '10, Ryan Peacock '09, Rob Sherry '10,
Peter Bauleke '10, Andy Wassel '08, Nick Vandam '09, Andy Cahoy '10,
Nick Dason '07, Nicholas Sterghos '09*

stimulus). Or, pacing while most are going out fast. Finish in the middle of the pack while some are trying to finish first.

Why: Because if you finish first with a high heart rate and a body full of lactic acid, the person who finished in the middle of the pack with a low heart rate and no lactic acid will catch you on a bike in about 90 seconds—and keep on going.

Strategy: Relax.

Why: Gennady Touretsky—Alexander Popov's coach—said, "Relaxation at high speeds is the most important factor in winning workouts, races, and Olympic gold medals." Popov won four golds and a silver—one of which, a gold, he gave to his coach (in case you're wondering what to give Major Van Atta before you graduate). But for now, give yourself a 130 heart rate when you get out of the water. It'll be worth gold during the bike and run.

*Nick Dason '07, Dora,
Ryan Peacock '09, Andy Cahoy '10*

Practice

Tuesday, 21 March
90 minutes, 4,200 yards.

Dryland discussion (5 minutes)

Tonight is all about pacing. You want to be able to hold a pace in a race for 1500 meters. We'll approximate that by holding a pace for 50-100-200 and 500 yards at a time, giving you a chance to think—in between sets—about how you will modify your stroke length and rate, as well as what you will focus on to hold the pace.

Warm-up, finding pacing lane. (10 minutes, 500 yards)

Pacing Segment:

3x: 50-100-150-200. You want to keep the same pace for each segment. Check your time after each segment. One minute rest between each cycle. (30 minutes, 1,500 yards)

2x: 5x100 at your pace. (five breaths' rest between 100s)

500 at your pace. (40 minutes 2,000 yards)

Cool down 10 minutes or until 19.50

Post-practice/Race discussion: 10 minutes

Ryan Peacock '09, Nick Dason '07, Nick Vandam '09,
Peter Bauleke '10, Rob Sherry '10, Bryan Lagasse '10

Practice

Friday, 24 March
38 minutes, 1,900 yards.

This morning is all about pacing. You want to be able to hold a consistent pace in a race. We'll approximate that by holding a pace for shorter distances, giving you a chance to think—in between sets—about how you will modify your stroke length and rate, and what you will focus on to hold the pace.

Warm-up, find pacing lane. (10 minutes, 400 yards). Get in a lane with someone who swims at the same pace. Crowd into lanes. Drafting is good. Think NASCAR. Think cycling.

Pacing Segment:
50-100-150-200. You want to keep the same pace for each segment. Check your time after each segment. 10 breaths between each segment. Keep your heart rate at 150 or less. Rotate lane leaders. (10 minutes, 500 yards)

500 at your pace. (8 minutes 500 yards). Be as consistent as possible.

Cool down. (10 minutes – 500 yards)

Stay long in the water. This means take fewer strokes. Stroke count for each 25 yards should be three less at the cool down than at the warm up

When you think you are cooled down, swim one length (25 yards) underwater taking a normal breath at the beginning. You should reach the end of the pool easily and not out of breath. If you can't, you aren't sufficiently cooled down. Your heart rate before doing this should be 110 or less.

How You Think Determines
How You Perform

or

Stalking the Elusive Thought Pattern

by Laurie Ferguson, Ph.D.

Training, drills, practice, practice, practice. That is what conventional coaching teaches is the key to high performance. "Build your muscles and develop your lung power." "Master a better stroke with more pull." But excellence in performance requires a mental component along with the development of the body. How you choose to think and the control and discipline you bring to your mental training has an enormous impact on how well you can perform.

What are you thinking about when you jump into the water?

Just as important—what are you thinking when you are getting dressed to swim, when you are on your way to the pool, after practice is over? What goes through your mind as you swim set after set?

In training, you dissect your stroke, taking it apart moment by moment in order to see what you do and then correct it so you get the maximum speed and efficiency through the water. Your thoughts are as powerful as your muscles in creating and refining your stroke. Your thinking creates part of the energy that moves you forward or creates drag. Giving the same kind of attention to dissecting your thinking, thought by thought, helps you correct what holds you back and helps you maximize the thoughts that move you purposefully through the water.

It starts with watching what you think, paying attention over time to what content regularly flies through your mind, sometimes a little under the radar, or at least out or conscious awareness. With time and patient attention you can begin to track your thoughts. Maybe you begin to see that you are routinely critical of yourself. You call yourself names or ruminate on mistakes you make. Perhaps you are an inner complainer. You feel victimized by people or events. Why is this always happening to me? Or you realize you are usually optimistic about what is happening; you look on the bright side and feel everything will be ok. Noticing and being aware of what you think gives you useful information.

It takes time and commitment to get a clear picture of your thought patterns. We often resist knowing what we think—there are many ways to avoid paying attention to our quiet but persistent inner routines. But identifying what goes through your mind when you are doing a workout, going to practice or getting ready to compete is the first step towards harmonizing your physical and mental energy and increasing your power.

Mental Workout for Thinking

The easiest way to track thoughts is to feel your way into them. The quality you want to have is feeling good. Your thoughts will follow those feelings.

- Remember a time when you felt wonderful—energetic, focused, confident.

- Let yourself remember that time with all your senses. How did it feel in your body? How did it look, sound, smell, taste?

- What do you think about that time? When you are feeling good, hopeful, optimistic, free—you don't think critical or negative thoughts. What kind of thoughts were you having ?

Stage II

- When you are in a situation that has been stressful, slow your thinking down.

- Pay attention to what you are feeling—your mood, your attitude. If you are frustrated, begin to move towards the place where you feel a little freedom. Say you can't get a certain aspect of the stroke and you've been trying and trying. Your frustration could spiral towards anger and self-criticism. That can spiral down even further. But you are going to stop the spiral.

- Notice your feelings and your thoughts. Just observe.

- Reach gently in your mind for a feeling that is slightly better than frustration. Think about your kick or the way your hand is entering the water. Think about how your breathing is even or how your hips are staying afloat. You feel a little satisfaction.

- Let that feeling turn into thoughts about your swimming in the moment.

- Try the tricky part of that stroke again.

- You have just mastered a difficult thought process!

- Now repeat and repeat and repeat. Your real mastery will come with thousands of small but consistent repetitions.

Bryan Lagasse '10 and John Dubiel '08, U.S. Naval Academy midshipman who trained with the West Point Tri team while he was an exchange student

Bryan Lagasse '10

Erin King '08, Nick Haines '08

Tracy Wilson '07, Ashley Morgan '10, Emily Sfeir '09, Cristin Browne '09,
Erin King '08, Erica Triebenbach '10, Christine Kawoczka '08

Points to Work On

Wednesday, 29 March

```
From: Snipes, A
Sent: Wednesday, 29 March, 10:16
To: Louis Tharp
Subject: Re: Points to work on

Sir,

What should I work on next week? Thanks for your
help. I don't want to waste a week
without something to focus on. Talk to you soon.

Respectfully,
CDT LT Anthony Snipes
CO H2 Hornets
SWIM BIKE RUN - GO ARMY TRIATHLON
```

Ryan Peacock '09

Tony:

I hope you feel good about tonight. We've discovered the weak spots and the good news is that the solution isn't difficult to implement.

First, work on the surface tension drill. Don't fall into the typical overachiever frustration if it doesn't come easily. This is all about relaxation and balance. Start in a ball and extend the arms and legs at about the same time. At first just get horizontal in the water, even if you're not at the surface. Once you work out the right muscles to use to get horizontal, you'll have an easier time floating to the surface. Have fun with this. Swim a little and then try it again. You're using every muscle in your body to do this, but they're not being used in the usual way. The large muscles will be tensed—calves, quads, hamstrings, psoas, glutes, abs, pecs, deltoids, traps. But it's the stabilizer muscles in your core that will actually get you into position—iliopsoas, external and internal

abdominal obliques, triceps, levator scapula, iliotibial tract (IT Band), teres minor. http://www.over-achieversdiary.com/ref.cgi?1 (you can see front and back muscles by going to the left column menu. Click on the dots on the body to identify the muscles.)

Recruiting these muscles can be tricky at first because they often are subordinated by the larger

Andy Stock '10

ones. It's a mind/body exercise. When you attempt the drill, your mind has to figure out which muscles to recruit to make it happen. This means that, like all learning, it can take place after you first try and fail, then sleep, and then try again. Your brain will continue to figure out the puzzle while you're sleeping.

Second, work on the high elbow in and out of the water. High outside the water allows you to enjoy the benefit of gravity as your

Ryan Peacock '09, Peter Bauleke '10, Nick Dason '07, Nick Vandam '09

hand drops into the water—and helps move your shoulder over your arm, which helps the gliding process. High in the water, just before you are ready to take a stroke, recruits the bicep, tricep, lats and abs during the stroke. This means you're able to swim with the core body as well as with arm strength.

Nicholas Sterghos '09

When the elbow is dropped, the tiny shoulder muscles (rotator cuff muscles)—infraspinatus, supraspinatus, teres minor and subscapularis (see diagram link), are recruited to power the stroke. Swimming this way will tear them up over time. High elbow in the water also helps you to control your rotation. It is difficult to rotate 180 degrees with a high elbow because a high elbow naturally will set you up for the next stroke by keeping you from rotating too far. http://www.overachieversdiary.com/ref.cgi?2

Third, your rotation should be under control from doing the first two drills because you will not have to rotate as far for air. Once the balance issue is settled, it will be very easy to roll 45 degrees to air while keeping your body alignment (no thoracic twisting to get to air).

Fourth, head position. Look directly at the bottom of the pool. When you swim, think about a rope which is fastened to the top of your head pulling you through the water. Your head will be in line with your body, which means you'll be looking at the bottom of the pool. Why do you need to look at the bottom? When you raise your head your hips drop. Your head is like a bowling ball and raising it even a little bit transfers weight to your hips, lowering them in the water. When this happens, drag is increased dramatically. Of course, this is all about balance again. Your body needs to be a cylinder in the water. This means head, shoulders, and hips are all at the top of the water and above it. You want to feel water at L-4, L-5, and at the small of your back, just before it flows over your hips. This may take a while to experience, but when you do, you'll be experiencing balance in the water.

This is pretty advanced stuff. I can't tell you enough that it's a mind/body challenge, and you've got to be having fun while you're learning it in order to focus—no stress, no wandering thoughts. You're a very good swimmer now. We're talking about improvements that a lot of people will not experience, so do not get obsessed with this. Provide the best environment for the learning take place. Let success come to you—don't chase it. Every drill is connected; swimming is one of the few sports that allows you to nuance your way to success with conscious realization of what's happening.

Work on all these things at Tuesday's practice, but do me a favor and don't do the surface tension drill. I need to introduce the team to it first.

Let me know how you're doing. I'll be on email while I'm in Florida. Tell me if something's not working or doesn't make sense. We will find another way to achieve the same result. Your enthusiasm and focus is great.

Nick Dason '07

Can You Control Your Thoughts?

by Laurie Ferguson, Ph.D.

How smart are you?

Pretty smart—certainly above-average intelligence if you are a triathlete. This is considered a demanding sport—both physically and mentally. The physical aspect of the training is usually well covered. The mental aspect gets a little less attention.

Which is a mistake because mental skills give you a serious competitive edge.

So what kind of mental skills? You probably already know that you need a plan to compete. You have to think through contingencies: accidents, weather, unexpected conditions on the land or in the water, and have back up maneuvers and options. But psychological training involves more. To deal with the demands of training and competition and, to keep yourself motivated and on track, you need to examine what you are thinking, and how you use your mind.

Most of us don't work at controlling our thoughts or our consciousness. We assume that whatever thought enters our head, or whatever shiny object our attention is attracted to doesn't matter. We pay attention to what we put in our bodies—what we eat and drink, whether we're using organic sun tan lotion or particular vitamins and sport water. We make charts of our exercise and movements, and how much we sleep and how many calories we burn.

Yet we allow any amount of garbage to enter our minds. From advertisements to TV shows, to self-critical and demeaning inner comments, we let nonsense and untruths float along in our heads. We waste our valuable thinking time on minutiae or daydreaming about nothing.

To develop a hardy psychological state, fit for training and competing, requires mental effort, a willingness to understand and to practice techniques to improve our psychological fitness along with our physical workouts.

Mental skills include: regularly defining and understanding your motivation, using the elements that contribute to flow, visualizing, creating a workout and a competition script, using competition and team work to enhance your own performance, focusing, visualizing and mental goal setting.

You are a smart and dedicated athlete—that's why you want to learn more. Being willing to engage in something new with an open mind is one of the first keys to mental development. Strengthening your ability to pay attention and follow through with your mind before you engage your body will yield dividends in your performance and in your everyday practice.

Christine Kawoczka '08, Cristin Browne '09

Mental Workout to Visualize

- Choose a regular time of day that you will commit to practicing visualizing. This can be before bed, in the morning, in the shower, wherever. Make sure you have undisturbed privacy.

- Set aside ten minutes.

- Get comfortable.

- Choose something you want to practice—a stroke, balance, reducing drag.

- Decide if you want to feel it or see it yourself.

- Run the movie in your head—going over every detail.

- Run through it two more times. See or feel where the hesitation or difficult part is. Slow down and go through that part in slow motion.

- Do it again.

- Now switch. If you were feeling it, see it yourself. If you were watching it, imagine doing it.

- Practice that two more times.

- Make this part of your daily practice schedule. Isolate parts of your practice that you want to improve. Save those difficult moments to rehearse in your mental practice time.

- This practice is especially good for improving your focus and concentration. You can return to this mental state when you are in a competition and things are falling apart. Take a deep breath and remember how you did it in your mind. This mental practice can restore your confidence and balance, but only if you do it as a daily discipline.

John Leatherman '08

John Leatherman '08

Balance

Wednesday, 5 April

Within the mechanics practice sessions, we split the learning between glide, power and balance. This email talks about balance.

Tuesday we worked on balance. Why: Balance allows the power from your core, which is transmitted through your arms and hands to go towards propulsion—not to keeping you level in the water. Balance also allows you to remain streamlined, which means you will glide farther between power strokes.

Strategy: Pay attention to your hips through hip counts.
Why: We now want to move your focus from your arms to your

hips. Hips drive your stroke. They are the beginning of the kinetic chain which allows your whole body to propel you rather than just your arms/hands. Counting each time your hips twist allows you to feel the beginning of this power delivery system.

Strategy: Extract maximum forward motion from the glide part of your stroke.
Why: It's free. Your power stroke provides maximum

Erin King '08   acceleration. Once it is finished, you begin slowing. You want to preserve as much of this speed as possible, and the easiest way to do it is to reduce resistance. Keeping your body streamlined will preserve speed.

I will be swimming at Crandall Pool Wednesday night, 05 April, from 1830–2000. If anyone wants to join me I will be doing distance balance sets incorporating incremental speed increases up to balance threshold.

Practice

Tuesday, 4 April
90 minutes, 2,650 yards, plus cool down.

Warm-up: 300 yards.
2x:
   25 freestyle—extended weightless arm
   25 skating
   25 freestyle—extended weightless arm
   25 underskate
   25 freestyle—extended weightless arm
   25 zipper switch

Surface Tension Drill

Main set:
(2 minutes 100 yards)
   50 swim cruise pace (CP), for hip count by 25s
   50 fist swim for hip count by 25s
   Swimmers give hip count for fist and no fist.

(5 minutes, 250 yards)
   100 fist swim. Try to match CP swim hip count by 25s.
   150 fist swim. Match CP swim hip count by 25s.

(13 minutes, 700 yards)
2x:
   100 fist swim. Match CP swim hip count by 25s.
   150 fist swim. Match CP swim hip count by 25s.
   200 fist swim. Match CP swim hip count by 25s.
   250 fist swim. Match CP swim hip count by 25s.

Focal Points First Round:
   Kinetic chain
   Hip position

Kick
Focal Points Second Round:
Mail slot
Lead with elbow as long as possible
Hand position for anchor

(12 minutes, 600 yards)
200 freestyle for hip count/25 at perfect balance
1 minute rest
200 freestyle 25-yard hip count at perfect balance plus 10 percent speed
1 minute rest
200 freestyle 25-yard hip count at perfect balance plus 20 percent speed (if possible)

Cool down:
10 minutes freestyle, slow.

Andy Wassel '08, Andy Cahoy '10, Erica Triebenbach '10

Rob Sherry '10

All in before the Wildman Tri in Orlando. Andy Wassel '08,
Erica Triebenbach '10 back, Rob Sherry '10, Tracy Wilson '07, Peter Bauleke'10,
Ashley Morgan '10, Nick Haines '08, Dave Tyson '07 back, Ryan Peacock '09

Peter Bauleke '10

High Heart-rate Pacing

Tuesday, 11 April

Despite telling them that this was a descending set and to start out conservatively, the fast men did the first 50 in 34 seconds and the second 50 in 30 seconds. They did the 100 in 1:02. And their heart rate was close to 200. Now they knew exactly what it feels like to go out too fast. The rest of the team was more strategically oriented—or watched the fast guys and decided not to go there. The great part of this was that everyone learned from watching each other and then immediately implemented the right strategy for the set. It took the fast guys about 20 seconds to recover and then they were off again.

Emily Sfeir '09

Because everyone set personal intervals, I was able to talk to swimmers when they came in, give them focal points, and watch and comment as their strokes deteriorated. The lesson was that when they start to feel exhausted, that is the cue to pay attention to technique. The benchmark is hip count. As soon as it goes up, it's time to go through a focal point check list. Each swimmer did something counter-productive when they got tired—the most common was bad tracking and impatient hand. Two women literally raised their heads out of the water when they were exhausted—and their hips fell immediately along with their pace. Once they knew what their particular exhaustion focal point was, I could see them working to fix it.

The cool down was a 200 swim/active rest at 6 minutes with heart

> rate check. If heart rate was more than 130, they had to do another 100 at 2:30. Some didn't understand that the rationale for keeping the interval was to disperse lactic acid, bring heart rate down, and regain stroke confidence.
>
> The philosophy is to swim smart—in the warm up, the main set and the cool down.

Tuesday we worked on high heart-rate pacing. Why: The simple answer here is that you now know what it feels like to take off too fast. When you get the feeling in a race that you had tonight, decrease your hip count and focus on a patient hand. The less lizard-brained answer is that it gave me a chance to see some tired, raggedy strokes that resulted from high-heart rate swimming.

Strategy: Pay attention to your pacing, especially at the start of a race.
Why: Save yourself for the bike and run. It's about pacing, not about sprinting.

Strategy: Pick a few focal points to think about during practice/racing.
Why: It's all about managing your body in the water. Go through a check list while you're swimming:

- Is your head in line with your body? Visualize a rope coming out of the top of your head that is pulling you along. Your head must be in line with your body or the rope can't pull you.

- Are you keeping your arms and hands away from your body's centerline? Maximum power is produced when arms/hands do not cross the centerline

Nick Vandam '09

of your body, either in the water or out. It's impossible to reduce resistance when arms/hands are crossing the centerline of your body. The drill is to swim down the center line of the pool watching to make sure your arms/hands stay outside the black line.

- Are you allowing your arm to extend patiently so you can set up a good catch with downward facing hand and high elbow? You only get one chance to maximize power per stroke.

- Is your body a cylinder that slides through a single hole in the water? For

Bryan Lagasse '10

every increase in speed, resistance is cubed. Reducing resistance is the smart way to improve your glide between strokes in order to hold as much speed as possible before your next opportunity to maximize power per stroke.

- Zen tip: Author Sue Bender says, "Stop practicing struggling. Start practicing enjoying." Enjoyment in the water equals relaxed swimming, and relaxed swimming is fast, efficient swimming. Another way to look at it: if you're not fast, you're not relaxed.

Andy Stock '10

Practice

Monday, 10 April
minutes, yards.

Email to my coach, Terry Laughlin.

Terry:

Last night was a great practice because the fast boys were getting frustrated with pacing, so I gave everyone the following. There was also a team meeting so we only had 40 minutes for practice.

Warm-up:
   100 Slow slow quiet swim.
   100 Skate the right way. Focus on head position, breathing position, body as cylinder, relaxed hand on IT band.
   100 Underswitch.
   100 Shark fin with spearing, patient hand and solid anchor before the stroke.
   100 Fist swim in order to force proper high elbow position in the water.

Main set:
   50 for time and hip count
   50 descending time, constant hip count
   100 descending time, hip count plus 2 per 25
   200 descending time, hip count same as 100
   400 descending time, hip count plus 2 per 25 if necessary
   10 breaths between each

Repeat until 10 minutes before the end of practice.

Focused Pacing

Friday, 14 April

This morning, we revisited pacing—the most important strategy in the swim part of a triathlon—and we talked about how to keep focused.

Strategy: Focus and pacing are symbiotic.

Why: The idea behind pacing is to allow your body and mind to deal with a triathlon in an organized and confident manner. It allows you to manage your body and your expectations. The concept of focus is tricky to understand because there are really three

Mike Herndon '07

parts to it. The first is what everyone thinks is focus—a single-minded concentration on the task at hand with the conscious and unconscious mind dedicated to the correct completion of the task. The second part of focus is losing focus. Yes, the second part of focus is losing focus. The third part is beating yourself up for losing focus. Being focused and losing focus is human. Beating yourself up over losing focus is learned behavior and can be unlearned on the way to becoming a champion. If you think about fly fishing, it's easier to understand how the concept of focus and regaining focus works. A fisherman casts the line into the river and almost immediately it begins floating downstream. To counteract this, a simple wrist movement brings the line back upstream. The key here is that the fisherman expects the line to go downstream, away from where it was originally cast. If you think of focus as

Ryan Peacock '09, Nick Vandam '09, Peter Bauleke '10, Nick Dason '07,
Rob Sherry '10, Nicholas Sterghos '09, Bryan Lagasse '10, Erin King '08,
Total Immersion Multisport Director Greg Sautner, Nick Haines '08,
Louis Tharp swim coach, Dave Tyson '07, Cristin Browne '09, Andy Wassel '08,
Christine Kawoczka '08, Joe Imbriaco '07, Tracy Wilson '07, Ashley Morgan '10,
Erica Triebenbach '10, Andy Cahoy '10, Emily Sfeir '09

the line being cast, and losing focus as the line going downstream, it is easy to look at regaining focus as a simple matter of bringing the line back upstream—without a lot of drama. If you accept that you will lose focus, it is much easier to regain it and you don't waste time being angry over losing focus, which, of course, just makes you lose focus. For overachievers like yourselves, it's all about managing your body and your expectations so you can deal with a triathlon in an organized and confident manner.

Strategy: Stay sensitive to stroke degradation.

Why: If you are able to notice when your stroke is falling apart, you can focus on employing the fix quickly. Common areas where stroke degrades:

- Patient hand becomes impatient. If you are spearing your hand into the water and immediately taking a stroke, you are losing glide speed and power. Let the hand hang out for a second so you maximize the glide, and set up for an efficient catch and powerful stroke.

- You start looking where you want to go. Sounds like it's the right thing to do, but when you look forward, your head comes up—and when your head comes up, your hips fall. When your hips fall, so does your speed because in this lower position they increase resistance dramatically.

- You notice that your patient hand is turned up or flopping around before you start the power part of your stroke. Your underwater arm needs to be 30–45 degrees in relation to the surface and your hand needs to be pointing down. This allows you to get a maximum catch and a powerful stroke.

- You notice your arms are crossing the center line of your body. When your arms cross the center line of your body, your ability to incorporate your hips and core body muscles into your stroke is almost impossible. You want to swim with body power, not arm power, and

Christine Kawoczka '08

keeping your arms outside the center line helps you do this.

Rob Sherry '10

Practice

Friday, 14 April
60 minutes, 2,500 yards, plus cool down.

Warm-up: 500 yards. (heart rate at end of warm-up <130)
100 freestyle—fist swim—focus on high elbow in the water
100 freestyle—full hand swim—focus on high elbow in the water
100 freestyle—patient catch—extended arm, dropped hand, solid catch
100 freestyle—fist swim—focus on high elbow in the water
100 freestyle—full hand swim—focus on high elbow in the water

Main set: 2,000 yards (heart rate <150)
2x:
5x 100
First 100 is for pace. Remember hip count and time.
Second–Fifth 100. Decrease time. Keep hip count under control: <3 extra hip counts per 25.
1x 500
Take lowest time and hold it for 500. Use hip count from best 100.

Focal points:
Glide through a single hole in the water
Quiet swimming
High elbow
Patient catch

Cool down:
10 minutes freestyle, slow. (heart rate <130)

Core Body Balance

Wednesday, April 26

Tuesday, we talked about balance and keeping your whole body involved in swimming. Swimming is not about your arms. It's about your core body. The hips drive the stroke. We also talked about focal points you can use this summer during uncoached training.

Strategy: Give drills your complete attention. A drill allows you to isolate the specific skill necessary to achieve successful whole-stroke swimming. If you don't know why you're doing a drill, ask. Never do a drill, or a practice for that matter, that doesn't make sense to you.

Why: Every drill we do is directly connected to swimming. Drills allow your brain to work out what is necessary to be efficient, one focal point at a time. If the drills make sense and you can see how they help your swimming, they will help your swimming.

Strategy: Add controlled stress during your practice in order to test your ability to keep a whole stroke together. Also, give yourself an opportunity to think about how to improve your stroke.

Why: By doing a 100, 200, 100, 300, 100, 400, 100, 500, at race pace, you introduce stress in measured amounts. This allows your body and your mind to accept the stress and process it. The

Nick Dason '07

100s, also swum at race pace, allow you to think about how to manage your body during the longer sets. The longer sets allow you to apply what you have learned. These are high-stress sets, but they give you a psychological advantage over an actual race because you have the 100s to rethink your swimming. Next week we may reduce the amount of yardage for rethinking and add more race-stress swimming. The objective is to familiarize you with race stress. Familiarization lowers stress during a race.

Strategy: Use your personal focal points.

Why: Everyone is great at certain aspects of freestyle and weak at others. Some need to work on tracking, others need to work on a patient hand, hip connection, resistance reduction, or breathing. Knowing your focal points gives you the opportunity to maximize your practice, imprinting the correct stroke mechanics into muscle memory, and allowing your swimming to consistently improve. Practice makes permanent. If it is done right, practice makes perfection permanent.

Andy Wassel '08

Practice

Tuesday, 25 April
60 minutes, 2,200 yards, plus cool-down.

Warm-up: 400 yards
- 50 swim
- 50 left hand lead with emphasis on balance—body is horizontal
- 50 right hand lead—same emphasis
- 50 underswitch—emphasize tracking
- 100 fist swim with hip count by 25. notice high elbow throughout power stroke and long glide
- 100 swim—emphasizing high elbow during the power stroke, and long glide at race pace

Main set: 1,800 yards
100
200
100
300
100
400
100
500

Tracy Wilson '07

All to be done at race pace. 10 breaths between each.

Purpose: The 100s allow you to reset your stroke. The graduated distances push you to keep a consistent pace, heart rate and hip count.

Cool-down: 500 yards. (heart rate at end of cool-down <130)

Mike Herndon '07, unidentified non-tri-team competitor

Ryan Peacock '09, Joe Imbriaco '07

Summer Take-Away Practice

Wednesday, May 3

> *The last practice of the season is always good and bad. It's good because the team has the opportunity to distinguish between discipline—showing up for practice, and self-discipline—practicing alone. This concept of discipline vs. self-discipline was being taught long before I got to West Point. It is one I like and I use it to help determine who the champions are.*

Tuesday evening's practice was the Summer Take-Away Practice with an individual sustain/improve assessment from TI coach and All American swimmer, Stefan Bill. This email covers what you can do over the summer. A separate email will review the sustain/improve points from Stefan's assessment, as well as mine over the past nine practices.

Action: Consistent Correct Swimming
Why: Swimming correctly and often is the only way to learn—and when you learn, you improve. Every time you get in the water, you need to learn something new about swimming by focusing on technique at or below race pace. Move into race pace plus when you can hold your stroke together. Doing this will get you to a new race pace.

Peter Bauleke '10 back,
Ryan Peacock '09 back,
Bryan Lagasse '10 side

Action: Know where you are on the competency chart.
Why: Understanding where you are on this chart will help you get to the next level. Here are the levels:

Unconscious Incompetence—This describes many swimmers who don't know how badly they are swimming. Nobody on the tri-team is in this category.

Conscious Incompetence—This is when you know you are making mistakes but you don't know how to correct them.

Conscious Competence—This is when you stop making mistakes and you know you're swimming correctly.

Unconscious Competence is when you're swimming correctly and you're not thinking about it.

Most of you will be in the conscious competence category, and it's important not to worry about getting to the unconscious competence level. It is, however, important not to fall into the conscious

Peter Bauleke '10, Ryan Peacock '09

incompetence category—and this is easy to do. Your first indication that you might be slipping is when swimming becomes boring and you don't feel like you're progressing. You get the sense that there's a problem with your stroke, but you can't identify what needs to be fixed. What do you do? Go back to the drills. Take your time. Remember how slowly Stefan warmed up Tuesday night. His drills were deliberate and careful—not fast. Head lead, hand lead, underswitch, overswitch, fist swim. Pay attention to what is happening. Be open to learning while you're doing the drills and in subsequent swimming. Often just doing the drills will reawaken your muscle memory and your stroke will improve. Send me an email if you're stuck. Tell me what's happening. I probably know your strokes well enough to get you moving in the right direction.

Action: Join a swim team

Why: You will swim. However, don't use fins, pull buoys, kick boards or any other toys except fist gloves. Rely on your own power and sense of balance. Don't do extended kick sets or pull sets. Swim in a pool or in open water, but swim. Your swimming should focus on technique not speed. Your speed will increase as your technique improves. The speed will come to you. Don't chase it or your stroke will fall apart. Move your race pace into fast territory by reducing drag, swimming more efficiently, and paying attention to technique.

Nick Vandam '09

Action: Think about your focal points while swimming.

Why: Keeps you aware of your efficiency. General focal points are: reducing drag, high elbow in power stroke, tracking, quiet swimming, gentle kick, and patient hand. If you swam with Stefan tonight you'll get your own focal points in an email. Be consciously competent.

Action: Tell me where you'll be this summer.

Why: I travel a lot and I swim a lot. We can work out together.

Action: Every two weeks swim a 200 meter or yard freestyle for hip count by 25 and time and email results to me.

Why: I will track your progress, and help work out stroke questions. I will be traveling in the U.S. Canada and Europe over the summer. So far, I know I will be in Memphis, Montreal, San Francisco-Silicon Valley, Chicago, and Baltimore. If you want to work out this summer send me your location and if I'm there, I will let you know.

Practice

Tuesday, 2 May
60 minutes, 2,500 yards, plus cool-down.

Warm-up: 500 yards

- 100 fist swim - hip count by 25s, gentle kick, notice high elbow in the water. 50 left hand lead with emphasis on balance—body is horizontal.
- 100 swim - hip count by 25s, gentle kick, focus on high elbow in the water.
- 50 underswitch—emphasize tracking and high elbow in the water.
- 50 overswitch—emphasize tracking and high elbow in the water.
- 100 fist swim - hip count by 25s, gentle kick, notice high elbow in the water.
- 100 swim - hip count by 25s, gentle kick, focus on high elbow in the water.

Main set: 1,000 yards x2

(We will be noting specific sustain/improvement focus points, both relaxed and under stress.)

- 50 for hip count
- 100 race pace
- 50 hip count
- 100 race pace plus—just before stroke falls apart
- 50 hip count
- 150 race pace
- 50 hip count
- 200 race pace plus—try not to let stroke fall apart
- 50 hip count
- 200 race pace

10 breaths between each.

Purpose: The 50s allow you to reset your stroke. Your hip count should remain the same for each 50. The graduated distances and increased speed will increase heart rate and tax your stroke. We will be able to note sustain/improvement. Stefan and I will talk to you about stroke mechanics during your practice. Stefan will also be swimming with you to match your strokes and talk about what he sees in the water.

All in before the race. Everyone notices when Army Tri arrives.

Volleyball time.
Dave Tyson '07, Rob Sherry '10

Practice

Tuesday, 9 May
60 minutes, 2,300 yards, plus cool-down.

Warm-up 500 yards:
- 200 swim - hip count by 25s, gentle kick, notice high elbow in the water. 50 left hand lead with emphasis on balance—body is horizontal.
- 50 underswitch—emphasize tracking and high elbow in the water.
- 50 overswitch—emphasize tracking and high elbow in the water.
- 100 fist swim - hip count by 25s, gentle kick, notice high elbow in the water.
- 100 swim - hip count by 25s, gentle kick, focus on high elbow in the water.

Main set 1,700 yards:
(We will be noting specific sustain/improve focus points both relaxed and under stress.)
- 50 for hip count
- 200 race pace
- 50 hip count
- 200 race pace plus—just before stroke falls apart
- 50 hip count
- 250 race pace
- 50 hip count
- 300 race pace plus—try not to let stroke fall apart
- 50 hip count
- 300 race pace
10 breaths between each.

Purpose: The 50s allow you to reset your stroke. Your hip count should remain the same for each 50. The graduated distances and increased speed will increase heart rate and tax your stroke.

Cool-down:

10 minutes of slow swimming and drills. Think about what you learned during your practice.

Nick Dason '07

Cristin Browne '09

Ryan Peacock '09, Peter Bauleke '10, Nick Vandam '09, Wolverine, Nick Dason '07, Andy Cahoy '10

Erin King '08, Christine Kawoczka '08, Tracy Wilson '07,
Cristin Browne '09, Emily Sfeir '09, Ashley Morgan '10

Officer in Charge LTC Ralph Vargas, Erin King '08, Nick Haines '08

Nick Dason '07, Nick Vandam '09.
These guys are number one and two; they're inseparable in
training and racing. Halfway through the '06–'07 season,
they became known as the VanDasons.

Finding Efficiency Through Reduced Resistance

Friday, 29 September

It was good to see all of you this morning—returning athletes and new ones. I'll learn everyone's name as soon as possible. Because time is short at practice, I'll send an email that reviews what we did, and elaborates on the reasons why. I'll cover the physical and the psychological components of each practice. Anytime you have questions, email me or let me know at practice.

Today's practice: Finding Efficiency Through Reduced Resistance.

Reducing resistance in the water equals free speed. Today we worked on the lower half of the swimming sine wave—the glide. This is the non-power segment—when one arm is extended and

the other arm is recovering. Everyone slows down during this segment. The objective is to lose as little speed as possible. Protecting your speed gives you two advantages. First, it takes much less power to maintain speed than to create it—so the less you slow down, the less you will have to work to regain speed on the power stroke. Second, your potential for increasing speed is greater when you carry speed into the stroke.

Tracy Wilson '07,
Erica Triebenbach '10

Physical component. Today's drill—the hand lead drill—was designed to reduce resistance in four areas.

• Head position. Keep your head in line with your body. Imagine a rope coming out of the top of your head pulling you down the pool. This will keep your head in line with your body. Water should be flowing over the back of your head. You should be looking directly at the bottom of the pool. If your head is high (you'll be looking at the wall or out in front of you if it is) your hips will drop, increasing resistance.

- Leading hand position. Arm in the water at 45-degree angle. Hand pointing downward. Yes, you will feel some resistance, and yes, this is not as slick as having your arm extended near the surface with hand pointed toward the wall. However, swimming is about trade offs. You lose some glide, but you gain balance and anchor position for the power stroke. (We'll talk about anchor position in two weeks when we work on the power side of the swimming sine wave. We'll talk about balance next Friday). For now, feel the water on the back of your hand and keep your arm at 45-degrees. It is important to keep the leading hand extended. This increases your body length and a longer body goes faster. If you extend your arm fully (at 45-degrees) you can add two feet to your body length. You will go faster because long boats go faster than short boats—it's free speed.

- Resting hand position. For this drill your other arm will rest on your side. This is so you can feel when your hand and arm (up to your elbow) is out of the water. If it is, your hips are high in the water, and high hips mean greatly reduced drag.

- Gentle kick. For triathletes, your kick is not about propulsion. Propulsion comes from your core body, but we'll talk about this in two weeks. Most triathletes' kicks are a source of drag. The best triathlon kick comes from the hips with very little knee flexion— and with feet pointed toward the wall

Nick Vandam '09

Erin King '08, Erica Triebenbach '10,
Christine Kawoczka '08, Tracy Wilson '07

(the bottom of your feet should face the ceiling). Think of how a Barbie doll's legs move. Very little knee flexion, all movement is from the hips. Your legs stay within your body line, reducing resistance.

• High hips. Low hips mean you are swimming uphill—the largest part of your body is impeding forward motion. Keeping your hips high in the water is critical for low-resistance swimming. Today, some of you began adjusting hip height through leading arm position. We will continue this next week when we discuss balance as another way to find efficiency through reduced resistance.

Many of you mentioned that this drill is easier on one side than the other. This is normal. It means you are more naturally balanced on the side where the drill feels easier. This is important for two reasons. First though, congratulations on listening to your body. It means you are sensitive to your movement in the water which is the first step in body management. Second, you can feel the effect drag has on your swimming, which is the second step in body management. You'll get to the point where you will consciously recognize drag and eliminate it as you swim while your competitors might unconsciously detect it and inappropriately apply muscle in an attempt to overcome it. Guess who will be better prepared for the bike and run?

Psychological component. Relax. Athletes often confuse the concept of relaxation during sport. For many, relaxation feels counterintuitive to performance. Relaxation in sport does not include La-Z-Boy® furniture, a TV remote, or any food product from

Dave Tyson '07,
graduated first in his class.

Lay's®. Relaxation in sport improves performance because it is primarily a psychological activity, not muscular. A good swimmer brings existentialism to the water—brings calm to chaos. At some points in your stroke your muscles will be relaxed, and at other times they will be stressed. Relaxation is the psychological paradigm that allows your muscles to achieve peak performance. It allows your brain to produce chemicals that contribute to competitive success instead of those that contribute to fear, panic and oxygen deprivation. A relaxed athlete is a champion. As I said last spring, Gennady Touretsky, Alexander Popov's coach said, "Relaxation at high speeds is the most important factor in winning workouts, races and Olympic gold medals." Popov won four Olympic golds and a silver for Russia, before Michael Phelps, and his coach Bob Bowman, proved Michael could relax even more, when he won six gold and two bronze medals at the 2004 Summer Olympics.

Practice

Friday, 29 September
50 minutes. Drill work.

Warm-up: 10 minutes slow freestyle. Heart rate <130

On-deck discussion: 10 minutes
- Finding efficiency through reduced resistance – sine wave
- Body management – appreciate in-water experience
- Hand lead drill discussion/instruction
  - Head position – rope analogy
  - Leading hand position – long boat analogy
  - Resting hand position – relaxed and above water
  - Gentle kick – within body area, Barbie doll analogy
  - High hips – basketball analogy
- Fist swim drill discussion/instruction
  - 25-yard swim for base stroke count
  - Continuous fist swim
    - Objective: match swim stroke-count
    - Forearm catch

All in before the swim.

Main set: 20 minutes
- Hand-lead drill facing white board
- Skill-based individual assessment to move to fist swim

On-deck discussion: 10 minutes
- Physical objective of practice – reduce resistance
- Psychological objective of practice – relax
- Two weeks – reducing resistance – lower sine wave
- Two weeks – increasing power – upper sine wave
- Swimming's role in a triathlon
  - A warm-up for the bike – finish with 120 heart rate
    - Save glycogen
    - Preserve mental freshness
    - The 90-second rule

Nick Vandam '09.
When you're one of the first out of the water, T-1 is a lonely place.

Drill Your Way To Happiness

Tuesday, 3 October

Hello Everyone:

Most people can't drive their Toyota® efficiently, and are intimidated at the thought of driving a Ferrari®—efficiently or not. They don't realize the potential of their car, from a fuel economy, driving efficiency, or mechanical systems preservation standpoint. They use the brakes too much, don't pay attention to tire pressure, drive looking at the end of their hood instead of taking a long view of the road, bring too much destructive emotion with them, and tend to look at driving as something to do while eating, drinking, talking on the phone, or spending quality time with their kids—missing the entire point of driving.

Most people can't swim efficiently either, and are intimidated by the thought of it. They don't realize the potential of their body from a physical, emotional, or energy preservation standpoint. They introduce resistance into their stroke, don't pay attention to breathing or balance, or they swim looking ahead. They bring too much destructive emotion with them to the pool and look at practice as something to slog through—missing the entire point of swimming.

It's no wonder there are so many bad swimmers. Look at all the bad drivers.

Connecting your emotions, judg-

Rob Sherry '10, Bryan Lagasse '10

ment, physical potential and logic will make you a better swimmer. I can't help with your driving, but luckily you don't need to be able to drive well to be a successful triathlete.

Swimming well is more a matter of breaking old habits. Learning new ones is easier.

Nick Vandam '09

There is a part of you that says "no" regardless of your actions—this part especially affects swimmers who already have a good grasp of technique, above average swimmers, and stubborn people. The U.S. Olympic Training Center has dealt with this issue in a several ways, none of them entirely successful. One interesting attempt to break old habits and overcome psychological and emotional resistance to new levels of speed was to tow a swimmer down the pool at world record pace. The theory, presumably, was to familiarize a swimmer with what it's like to go fast so the brain could connect with the body and make it happen without the tow rope. That's like jumping under a steam roller to get familiar with deep tissue massage.

There is a better way. Drills. But drills have a lot of problems with humans because humans don't naturally work and play well with drills. Coaches tell swimmers to do drills—but they don't instruct them about how or what. Fast swimmers can hate them because they think they have to go slowly, they're not usually aerobic, are boring, are stupid, and the person behind is usually running into the person in front. And, they usually involve kicking. Pretty much, drills are the flossing of swimming. There is no way to make flossing more appealing, but drills have the potential to become the foreplay of an efficient stroke. Or whatever.

Here's what drills do for swimmers:

- They get blood to your muscles by allowing you to warm up slowly at first and then allow you to move to race pace in a continuous pattern.

- They help your brain and body get reacquainted with the rules of efficient swimming.

Here's what swimmers do for drills:

- Give them a bad name.

It's a lopsided relationship so it's not surprising that it's dysfunctional.

In order to perform any athletic activity at maximum potential, your muscles have to be warm. This means there has to be an abundance of blood carrying oxygen to the muscles and carrying various waste gasses away. Without this, you enter that intriguing anaerobic state, that depending on your age, is a little like bad acid or good Percocet®. Either way, you won't be competing for long with cold oxygen-deprived muscles. It's also a waste of time to warm up—to get maximum oxygen flow to your muscles—without incorporating something else, such as drills. You have to warm up anyway, so why not use drills? Because here's what happens: as swimmers, the only thing we have in common with fish is our memories.

Nick Vandam '09

Peter Bauleke '10

That's right, you saw *Finding Nemo*. The only funny part was when Ellen DeGeneres kept saying the same thing over and over again, courtesy of her seven-second-span of goldfish memory. Your swimming memory is a little better, but not much.

Triathletes have been running and biking for years, whether they've been competing or not. Swimming, not so much. Running and biking are all about a push to go faster, apply more energy and see the result immediately. Swimming, not so much. Then there's breathing and not being able to do it with your head planted underwater.

With as little comparative time spent in the water versus biking and running—and factoring in the fear issue that centers around breathing—there's no reason why a triathlete should assume that swimming is natural. You need to refresh and retrain constantly. Oh yea, drills do this.

The problem with drills is that we do the wrong ones for the wrong amount of time, for the wrong reasons, too slowly, and allow our neuromuscular systems to draw the wrong conclusions.

Drills must be custom. They must reinforce what you're doing right and emphasize what you are doing wrong so you can fix it before practice. They need to be done both at a virtual standstill and at race pace. They need to be the way you reboot during a race when your swimming world falls apart and you're sucking in the muddy water churned up by the feet belonging to the person who just passed you.

Your particular drill sequence must be constructed when I can see your stroke at resting and at maximum heart rate. You need to be able to continuously reinforce the proper technique as well as test for the wrong technique during your drill

Ryan Peacock '09

sequence. After a drill sequence, you should be saying to yourself, "OK, what's my practice? I'm ready to swim," because talking to yourself is part of your drill sequence. We talk to ourselves constantly. The only way to tell if we're crazy is to examine what we're saying, not that we're doing it. If Ralph Waldo Emerson were a triathlete in addition to a poet and essayist, he would have said, "You are the kind of swimmer you tell yourself you are during drills," but instead he said, "A man is what he thinks about all day long."

Nicholas Sterghos '09, Jim Bumgardner coach Tharp's partner, Peter Bauleke '10, swim coach Louis Tharp

Your drills are all about maximizing efficiency, balance and speed. You begin a drill sequence with balance, then move to efficiency and then to speed. So when you see someone jump in the water and start swimming at something close to race pace, you know that's the person you are going to beat in the next triathlon—probably during the bike when that big lead coming out of the water disappears about 90 seconds past the transition area.

Because all drills are custom, it's impossible—without seeing your stroke—to tell you what drills to do. I'm not going to list them because you'll do them incorrectly, you'll do the wrong ones, and you'll end up still hating drills. Instead, we're going to talk about what they do and we'll agree during practice on the drills, their order, what they do, and their importance.

The first drills are for balance. Balance is critical in sport. The difference between balance in the water and on land is the water part. Water isn't as blunt as earth. When you pound water it moves out of the way. When it moves out of the way, you sink. When you sink you get nervous. Water responds to the lighter touch compared with earth. So it's easier to understand water when you compare it with air, not earth. Compared with air, water is highly

Joe Imbriaco '07, Nick Haines '08,
Christine Kawoczka '08, Erin King '08, Ashley Morgan '10

resistant and buoyant. Think of the effort you put into being streamlined on your bike. That's the mindset that will be successful in the water when you're trying to achieve balance, efficiency and speed.

Balance is all about staying on the top of the water. It's about keeping your entire body in a single horizontal plane—hips, feet, head, shoulders, and abs. If your hips and legs are dragging, you're swimming uphill. If you head is raised and you're looking ahead, your hips will drop, and you'll still be swimming uphill. If your body is not streamlined, your stroke not balanced, and your alternate side breathing not fully integrated into your stroke, you won't swim in a straight line. Worst case—you're swimming uphill, crooked, and a wetsuit won't save you.

But you're a sinker, you say. There is no way you can be horizontal in the water. Well, you were once—but you were horizontal about a foot below the surface. The only way you achieve any kind of floatation—forget about balance—is when you put your wetsuit on. In fact, you schedule your competitions so wetsuits are allowed.

Wetsuits provide buoyancy. If you can't get buoyant without a wetsuit, you're not only not balanced, but you're not swimming efficiently or as fast as you can. This means you'll be rolling into T-1 with a high heart rate and half-depleted glycogen when the volunteers are breaking out their bag lunches. The reason you sink is because you aren't relaxed in the water and you aren't going fast enough. We'll get to the "fast enough" part later. Your muscle mass plays a role, but there are triathletes with high muscle mass who float. They are relaxed. Relaxation in the water can

Mike Noel '07

be difficult. Check for tension in your hands and neck. Everything should be relaxed. Check what you're saying to yourself. Talk about relaxing in the water. Do the static balance drill. Think of your chest as a basketball. When you push a basketball into the water, it pops up. You can't keep it down because it has air in it. Practice this by pressing on various parts of your chest and watch for the water to provide resistance. Stand on a kick board in the water. Understand the small stabilizer muscles you need to recruit in order to stay on the kickboard. Try to translate these movements to your horizontal position. We'll do this more in practice.

Get mentally balanced. When you pass through the door to the pool, everything that doesn't help you swim gets left in the hall. This is not the place for extraneous worries or concerns, anger, or frustration. This is the place you swim. This is the sanctuary where learning takes place every time you get in the water. This is where you "aim for success, not perfection," because as Dr. David M. Burns goes on to say, "never give up your right to be wrong because then you will lose the ability to learn new things and move forward with your life." Being mentally balanced allows you to be wrong and successful at the same time—in or out of the water. Being physically balanced allows you to be efficient and fast at the same time—in the water.

Yea, I have no idea who Dr. David M. Burns is either. I found his quote a long time ago and I like it.

Next practice: efficiency and speed drills. Stone skipper will become your best friend.

Cristin Browne '09

Practice

Tuesday, 3 October
135 minutes. Drill work.

Warm-up: 10 minutes slow freestyle. Heart rate <130

Practice Summary:
- Finding efficiency through reduced resistance – lower half of the sine wave
- Body management – appreciate in-water experience
- Hand lead drill discussion/instruction
  - Head position – rope analogy
  - Leading hand position – long boat analogy
  - Resting hand position – relaxed and above water
  - Gentle kick – within body area, Barbie doll analogy
  - High hips – basketball analogy
- Fist-swim drill discussion/instruction
  - Objective: match swim stroke-count
  - Emphasize forearm catch
- Low resistance full-stroke swimming

Main set: 95 minutes
- 200 yards. Hand-lead drill, body facing white board
- 25 yards for base stroke count
- 5x 100 yards fist swim. Achieve base stroke count
- 5x 100 yards fist swim. Lower stroke count by 1 per 25
- 5x 100 yards fist swim. Lower stroke count by 5 per 100
- 1x 100 yards fist swim for time, holding last stroke count.
- 1 minute rest
- 5x 100 yards full-hand swim (no fist swim) descending time holding last fist-swim stroke-count (with 15 seconds rest/100)

Cool down: 10 minutes
- 200 yards. Hand-lead drill, body facing white board
- 25 yards relaxed underwater swim with strong push off

On-deck discussion: 10 minutes
- Physical objective of practice—reduce resistance
- Psychological objective of practice—relax
- 9/29–8/6—reducing resistance—lower sine wave
- 8/13–8/20—increasing power—upper sine wave
- Swimming's role in a triathlon
  - A warm-up for the bike—finish with 120 heart rate
    - Save glycogen
    - Preserve mental freshness
    - No need to finish first in the swim

*Faces: Andy Wassel '08 side, Mike Noel '07, Kari Vahle '09,
Nick Dason '07, Peter Bauleke '10 side*

The Magic of Flow

by Laurie Ferguson, Ph.D.

You've felt it – you were swimming along and suddenly everything opened up. It didn't seem like you were expending effort. Everything that needed to happen happened without your conscious effort or control. Maybe you were swimming hard and you felt your lungs about to explode—or maybe it was calm and you felt you were moving almost slowly, but it was your best time ever. Some people call this "being in the zone." Others describe it as a change in consciousness.

Researchers know it as the state of flow.

The term "flow" was coined by Mihaly Csikszentmihalyi, a psychologist who studies motivation and achievement. He observed that sometimes when people were fully absorbed and concentrating on something they were doing, something close to magic happened.

They had an altered consciousness and were powerful, efficient and effective without straining or stress. They felt deep enjoyment and pleasure in their activity.

Many athletes, particularly runners and swimmers, have a feeling of flow. Some athletes talk about flow as a peak experience, a spiritual moment when you feel fully alive.

This doesn't have to happen by accident. You can prepare the way for those heightened moments of enjoyment and transformation.

So how do you get there—and how do you get back once you've been?

The primary components of flow are concentration, preparation and pleasure.

Being in the present moment and focusing on what is happening now is the framework for flow. Paying attention to small details, you can tweak and control and enjoy it.

At times we swim with half a mind; we're rehearsing a conversation or going over a problem. We're thinking about dinner and what we need to do later. Our mind isn't on the stroke, the sense of moving in the water. There is no psychic flow possible.

But then there are days when we are in the stroke, we are in the kick, and we only exist to be right here doing this.

That is the mindful place for flow.

To make such a space, you adjust your awareness of what is around you. You don't get distracted. You let go of the mind chatter about how well you're doing or not doing. You stop evaluating yourself. You become unaware of the swimmer next to you, and the water temperature doesn't matter.

Your mind isn't on the goal—the press to win. Your mind is on the task at hand. What do you need to do to make your hands enter the water perfectly? How can you get a bit more juice out of your core?

You discipline yourself to that level of attention to detail. Then you open a space to flow.

Being prepared with a well-rehearsed game plan helps. When you have gone through what you need to do often enough that you can go into autopilot, you have made a flow pathway.

And don't neglect enjoyment.

Can you feel the pleasure of your muscles moving in rhythm, the harmony of leg and arm and breathing, the joy of exertion for its own sake? When we enjoy what we are doing and find fulfillment in it, just because, then the magic of flow begins.

Being in flow offers opportunities for growth and happiness. Flow experiences contribute to your development as an athlete, and beyond that, expand your potential as a human being.

That's taking swimming to a new level!

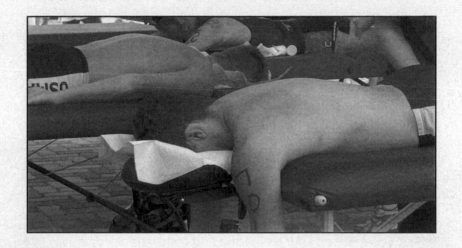

Mental Workout for Flow

We don't control when flow happens, but we can create the space or the pathway for that sensation of complete absorption and enjoyment.

Here are the elements that contribute to a flow state:

- Be prepared for practice or competition. Know what you need to do so you don't have to think about it. Mentally rehearse every aspect of what will occur from the moment you head towards body marking until you finish the race. Go over it until your whole routine is so familiar to you that it is automatic.

- Be present. Don't let your mind wander off into the fields of "after practice," "when I'm finished here," "tomorrow," "when I win," etc. Stay right here. You know that old sign at the bingo game—"Must be present to win"? That applies even more to flow. Notice what is around you this minute—look at the details.

- Smile. Yes—right now, smile to yourself. Think about what you enjoy in this sport. What is deeply pleasurable?

- Recall why you are doing this. What is your unique purpose for being a triathlete?

- Concentrate on your technique and competitive edge.

- Stay with what is happening and focus on the details and the pleasure of this moment. Does it feel delicious? Are you excited to be swimming? To be competing? Are you enjoying the water—the pull of your muscles, the exertion for this race?

These are the elements of flow. Over time as you prepare and practice they become second nature—and then you have even more potential to flow through the water—and to flow in your life.

Abstract Becomes Proficiency

Wednesday, 11 October

Last night everyone made some amazing conceptual and physical improvements. Your willingness to accept abstract thoughts regarding power generation, including power's correlation to gliding/reducing resistance, resulted in technique/speed breakthroughs that will become permanent with practice. We will continue to work out the practical application of these rules and theories in the water over the next few weeks. The objective is to allow you to construct an efficient, customized, winning swimming style. Congratulations on a very productive practice.

I've attached the powerpoint notes from last night's classroom session as this week's why email.

I won't be at Friday morning's practice, so I will email sets which will focus on these same concepts. Bring water.

I'll be holding in-water coaching Mondays and Wednesdays from 1830 to 2100. You can swim for any length of time, get questions answered, and work on specific technique/speed areas. Bring water.

As usual, let me know if you have questions or comments.

Speed = Power − Drag

Why Glide?

- It's a triathlon
- It's free speed
- It's the cube root
- It's how you stay fresh mentally
- It's how you stay fresh physically
- It's 1/3 of your warm-up

"It's the cube root" refers to drag vs. power.
Resistance increases by a factor of nine when power is applied.

Glide Points

- Head position
- Hand position
- Kick
- High Hips position
- Walls
- Breathing

"Walls" means how streamlined and powerfully you push off from the wall when you turn.

How You Know You're Gliding

- Stroke count
- Interval
- Heart rate

How You Know You're Not Gliding

- Car in snow—no traction
- Bug on windshield—massive resistance

Each Movement is Multi-task

- Every movement that reduces drag also can be used to increase power
  - Body Rotation
  - Long in the water
  - Quiet swimming
  - Kick within body line

Power Generating System

- Your core generates power. Swimming is a core power sport
  - Baseball
  - Tennis
  - Skiing
  - Golf
  - Roller Blading

Power Delivery *System*

- Arms
- Legs

  Power generation here leads to injury

Enabling Power

- Gliding prevention
  - Wandering hand
  - Wild Kick
  - Low hips
  - Twisted breathing
- Balance
  - Same as above

Existential Swimming

- Existentialism
  - Bringing order to chaos
- Existential Swimming
  - Bringing balance to power

Bringing Balance to Power

- Core stabilizer muscle development
- Neuro-muscular training
  - Practice makes permanent

Balance Training

- Stork bend
- 90-degree toe touch
- Sit-ups
- Exercise ball routines
- Unstable platform routines
- Static balance drill

New Warm-up Habits

- Resistance reduction drills
- Balance drills
- Power swimming

Power from the Core

- Body moves past your shoulders
- Stretch to the hip is the beginning of the stroke
- Stroke is straight back, high elbow—no S
- Kick is at the top of the power curve
- The speed your leading hand enters the water is the speed of your stroke
- Stroke stops in the hand lead position for anchor

Hips Are Critical

- Most triathletes don't use hip power
- The secret:
  - Power comes when hips move forward on a vertical plane, not through rotation
  - Hips control the kick and the stroke
  - Hips allow your body to move past your shoulders
  - Hip count is critical count for power. Stroke count is critical count for gliding.

Power from hips is critical. Most triathletes don't do it.
Unfortunately it is impossible to explain in a book.

Elbows Are Critical

- High elbow in the water = high speed
- High elbow out of the water = high speed

Patient Hand is Critical

- Anchor for maximum catch
- Position for maximum kinetic energy transfer

Review

- Power comes from the core
- Bring balance to power
- Without gliding, there is no speed

Practice

Friday, 13 October
50 minutes. Power drill work.

Warm-up: 10 minutes, 200 yards.
- Hand lead drill, body facing white board. Fist swim, Overswitch drill. Heart rate <130

Main set: 30 minutes
- 50 yards for base stroke count
- 4x 100 yd swim. Hold base stroke count/25. 15 secs rest
- 1x 100 yd swim for time, holding base stroke count
- 30 seconds rest
- 4x 100 yd swim. Descend time, hold base stroke count
  - Focus:
  - Forceful/deliberate hand entry at 45-degrees
  - Stretch from hand to hips with patient hand
  - Gentle kick
  - High hips
- Power ladder:
  - 100, 150, 200, 200, 150, 100. Hold stroke count, descend time on the back end

Cool down: 5 minutes, 200 yards
- Quiet swimming

Rob Sherry '10, Erin King '08, Dave Tyson '07, Christine Kawoczka '08,
Joe Imbriaco '07, Erica Triebenbach '10, Ryan Peacock '09,
Head Coach COL Pat Sullivan, Ashley Morgan '10, Nicholas Sterghos '09,
Peter Bauleke '10, Nick Haines '08, Bryan Lagasse '10, Tracy Wilson '07,
Andy Wassel '08, Nick Dason '07, swim coach Louis Tharp, Nick Vandam '09,
Cristin Browne '09, Total Immersion Multisport Director Greg Sautner

Erin King '08, Nick Haines '08

Emily Sfeir '09

More Power To You

Thursday, 19 October

Hi Team:

Here's the "why" email from Tuesday's practice. Sorry it's a day late. Life got in the way of coaching. I'm catching up, however, and Friday's practice is attached.

Friday morning's practice continues the "more power to you" theme. Enjoy it by being aware of what you're doing to allow your speed to increase.

But, back to Tuesday. The point is that when you started this season you were swimming as fast as you could. The question is: How do you get faster? The psychological answer is: Change your relationship with the water. The physical answer is: Change your stroke to allow increased glide, increased power generation from your core, and increased power delivery through your arms and hands. We focused on glide and now we're focused on power. With all due respect to Microsoft®, the important power point here is that the arms and hands are only the power delivery systems, not the power generating systems. Power comes from high elbow, accelerating hand/arm entry, and stretch to the hip—the core. As one hand is entering the water and accelerating, the other is doing what less enlightened swimmers call the

Tracy Wilson '07

"power stroke," but what we call the "power delivery stroke." It's your ability to accelerate your arm into the water, roll to your outstretched hand and recruit lats, abs and hips (the stretch, the core) that will transmit more power to the stroke.

Here's what was on the white board:

Glide review
Focal points:
- Head position—In line with your body
- Hand/Arm position—Arm 45-degrees, fingers pointing to bottom of pool
- Gentle kick
- High hips
- Early breathing

How you know you're not gliding:
   Stroke count increases
   Time increases
   Heart rate increases

Summary: Tired plus slow means pay attention to Drag. The solution is to focus on glide, not to add more power.

Power review
Focal points:
- Power comes from the core
- Body moves past your shoulders
- Arm accelerates into the water. The speed your leading hand enters the water is the speed of your stroke.
- Patient hand is critical
- Hips are critical
- High elbow is critical
- Hand entry away from the body center line (10 and 2 on the clock)

Practice

Friday, 13 October
50 minutes. Power and drill work. 1,800 yards.

Warm-up: 200 yds. 10 minutes. Hand lead drill, body facing white board. Fist swim, Overswitch drill. Heart rate <120.

Main set: 30 minutes
- 50 yards for base stroke count
- 4x 100 yd swim. Hold base stroke count/25. 15 secs rest
- 1x 100 yd swim for time, holding base stroke count
- 30 seconds rest
- 4x 100 yd swim. Descend time, hold base stroke count. 15 secs rest
- Focus:
  - Forceful/deliberate hand entry at 45-degrees
  - Stretch from hand to hips with patient hand
  - Gentle kick
  - High hips
- Power ladder:
  - 100, 150,150, 100. Hold stroke count, descend time on the back end. 8 breaths rest.

Cool down: 10 minutes, 200 yards.
- Quiet swimming. Hand lead drill.

Joe Imbriaco '07.
Coach K Award winner for outstanding leadership
as the Tri Team Cadet in Charge

Mike Noel '07

Body Management

Thursday, 26 October

Hi Team:

Tuesday night you were able to see your stroke as I see it. The video gave you the next clue to managing your body in the water. Next Tuesday we will record your underwater strokes so you can see what you're doing right and work on any movement that is not producing speed at a low heart rate.

If you were at the Total Immersion Swim Studio on Sunday, you had a chance to see underwater and above water video, as well as real-time feedback through the two mirrors in the endless pools.

And, the cadets who stopped by for Monday and Wednesday evening practice at Crandall were able to work one-on-one to imprint efficient swimming. (On Monday and Wednesday from 1830 to 2100 you can swim with me at Crandall. Some team members drop by for 20 minutes of low heart-rate instruction, and others put in an hour-plus practice. Match your needs to your schedule.)

The stroke improvement from Tuesday's and Sunday's videos is astounding. Everybody showed a dramatic improvement in body management—streamlining and power generation.

The group swim part of the practice provided insight into two areas—stroke limits and stroke recovery under stress.

The psychological part of the practice dealt with your ability to know that when your stroke falls apart in a race, you have the confidence that it can be fixed while you are racing. Physically, you have two choices when your stroke falls apart. You can either relax into a long glide, extending your patient hand for two seconds for five or six strokes and then go to a normal one-second patient hand, or you can speed up for five seconds before relaxing into a long glide with a patient hand for one second. Either activity will allow your brain/nervous system to reboot and get you back to low-stroke-count, low-heart-rate swimming. Your personality will determine which tactic you ultimately prefer, so try both.

Practice gave you the opportunity to isolate and process stress by swimming a 50 moderately, a 50 hard and an efficient 50 after reboot. The idea is to stress your stroke during the middle 50 and then put it back together so you are more efficient in the last 50 than the first 50.

Sometimes a set like this can upset your sense of continuity. We've worked on a smooth swimming style—both physically and psychologically—and forcing stress in the middle of a set can be unsettling. If you feel this way, the good news is that we won't do these short stress sets for long. Their purpose is to familiarize you with the sensation of an inefficient stroke and give you the tools— mentally and physically—to fix it. If your stroke falls apart in a race, it will be because you lost focus, you were hit by another swimmer, you veered off course, you're in choppy water, you're cold, you were thinking about something besides swimming, or fill-in-the-blank. Once you realize your stroke is off, I'd like you to be able to process the information calmly and implement a fix without guilt or panic.

Interestingly, when you feel a loss in continuity during a set like this, it means you are able to distinguish swimming from struggling and swimming feels better. This is a huge realization. Most of your competitors slog through the swim without any awareness of good vs. bad technique.

Friday morning's practice brings racing reality to the sets we began on Tuesday. Because the swim segment of a triathlon is all about pacing while racing, and because you know two of the three components of winning swimming—gliding and power generation—we want to explore the limits of your pacing abilities. If in the process your stroke falls apart, you'll be able to put it back together using the process we learned during the shorter sets on Tuesday. Practice is attached.

Oh yea, what's the third component? We'll begin to deal with it on Tuesday as we watch the underwater videos. It's balance. If you want to jump ahead, think gyroscope.

Practice

Friday, 20 October
50 minutes. Pacing While Racing.

Physical: Using gliding and power generation push yourself to a faster consistent pace. The key word is consistent.

Psychological: You want to feel like you're creating energy not consuming it. You want to know that if your stroke falls apart you can fix it.

Warm-up: 5 minutes. 100 yards. 100 hand lead drill, body facing white board. High hips. Anchored arm at 45-degrees. Heart rate <130. Relax.

Main set: 35 minutes. 1,800 yds. 15 calm breaths and think between each.
- 200 yards for base stroke count/25 at warm-up pace
- 200 yds. Focus: patient hand – comfortable pace
- 300 yds. Focus: hand entry acceleration – hold stroke count. Moderately fast pace
- 400 yds. Focus: Stretch to your hip – hold stroke count. Hold 300 pace
- 500 yds. Focus: High elbow, hand entry at 2&10, roll to patient hand – hold stroke count. Explore a faster pace and higher heart rate
- 200 yards for base stroke count/25. Holding 500 pace. Notice difference if any from the first 200

Cool down: 5 minutes
- 200 yards. Quiet glide swimming with minus 2 stroke count. (25-yd underwater swim to confirm low heart rate is optional.)

Practice

Friday, 3 November
50 minutes. Balance and Pacing.

Physical: Using information from your video, manage your body in the water to maximize balance with high hips, anchored patient hand and gentle kick.

Psychological: Visualize yourself as a gyroscope.

Warm-up: 5 minutes. 250 yards. 100 hand-lead drill, body facing white board. High hips. Anchored arm at 45-degrees. 150 balanced quiet swim. Heart rate <130. Relax.

Main set: 40 minutes. 1,700 yds. 15 calm breaths, and mentally confirm correct anchored hand position, especially when breathing. Be balanced and relaxed.

Do not count strokes.
- 200 yards at warm-up pace.
- 250 yds. Focus: patient hand, fingers down.
- 300 yds. Focus: hand entry acceleration, anchored hand, fingers down. Notice improper hand anchoring in other swimmers. Tell them—constructively.
- 350 yds. Focus: Stretch to your hip. Stretch your patient hand another three inches to lengthen your stroke.
- 400 yds. Focus: High elbow, hand entry at 2&10, roll to patient hand. Relax. Find a good rhythm.
- 2x100 yards. Now count your stroke. If you have swum the previous 1500 yards at a relaxed and balanced pace, your stroke count should be very low.

Cool down: 5 minutes
- 200 yards. Quiet glide swimming. (25-yd underwater swim to confirm low heart rate is optional.)

Practice

Tuesday, 14 November
120 minutes, 4,100 yards. Power and Pacing.

Physical: Using information from your video, manage your body in the water to maximize balance with high hips, anchored patient hand and gentle kick.

Psychological: Don't chase speed. Let it come to you.

Warm-up: 10 minutes. 300 yards. 100 hand-lead drill, body facing white board. High hips. Anchored arm at 45-degrees. 100 Underswitch. 100 Fist swim. Heart rate <130. Relax.

Main set: 80 minutes. 3,600 yds. Be balanced and relaxed.
- 500 yards at warm-up pace. Count strokes by 25s.
- 10x200 yds. Intelligently fast. +2 stroke/25. Descend.
- 500 yds. Focus: Hand entry acceleration, anchored hand, fingers down. Count strokes. Intelligently fast.
- 100 yds. Focus: Stretch to your hip. Stretch your patient hand another three inches to lengthen your stroke.
- 200 yds. Focus: High elbow, hand entry at 2&10, roll to patient hand. Relax. Find a good rhythm.
- 300 yards. Gentle kick. Visualize shoulders over arms.

Cool down: 5 minutes
- 200 yards. Quiet glide swimming. (25-yd underwater swim to confirm low heart rate is optional.)

Practice

Friday, 17 November
50 minutes. Power and Pacing.

Physical: Preparation for Tuesday's assessment. Intelligent fast pace.

Psychological: You will finish with a low heart rate (>140) because you know you can keep an intelligent pace, descending your times without losing stroke count control.

Warm-up: 5 minutes. 250 yards. 100 hand-lead drill, body facing white board. High hips. Anchored arm at 45-degrees. 100 underswitch. 50 balanced quiet swim. Heart rate <130. If you have custom drills, do them instead.

Main set: 40 minutes. 1,500 yds. Minimum. 15 calm breaths, and mentally confirm correct anchored hand position—especially when breathing. Be balanced and relaxed. This is your assessment trial run.
- 750 yds. Warm-up pace. Consistent low stroke count for "n".
- 500 yds. Intelligent race pace. n+1 stroke/25. Stretch with patient hand.
- 250 yds. Intelligent race pace. n+2 strokes/25. Descend time – should be less than half your 500 time.
- Check heart rate. (<140)
- Repeat as much of this as you can as many times as you can.

Cool down: 5 minutes
- 200 yards. Quiet glide swimming. (25-yd underwater swim to confirm low heart rate is optional.)

Bryan Lagasse '10, Andy Stock '10, Ryan Peacock '09

Mike Noel '07

Sinking to the Surface

Friday, 8 December

Hi Everyone:

A common problem among high muscle-mass triathletes is sinking. And while it seems to be true that some people are prone to sinking (and that often these people have high muscle mass) it's not productive to assume that because you have some bulk you are going to sink. It is more likely that you will sink if you are stressed. Fear, lack of confidence, and lack of technique cause stress and sinking. Before we go further, we need to separate stress from productive muscle tension. Productive muscle tension is when your arm and hand achieve maximum catch during a stroke utilizing core body strength. Stress is when your arm and hand aren't relaxed during the recovery. Stress wastes energy. Productive muscle tension turns energy into speed.

Notice how fast and erratically you are kicking. The faster and goofier your kick, the more stressed you are. Check your heart rate. It'll be high. A lot of times you'll revert to the leg motion of the sport you are most comfortable with when you're uncomfortable in the water. So if biking is your best event, you'll try to pedal in the water. Same with running. Neither of these works very well, however, except to define the goofy kick.

You can approach a sinking fix from either end of your body—

Nick Dason '07

your head or your feet. But it's primarily in your head—mass—and in your mind—stress. You can purposely slow down your kick, or you can intellectually and emotionally readjust your stress levels and your head position. Ultimately you'll do all three, but starting with the one you like the best helps speed the process.

If you start with your kick, it's most efficient and revealing to look at your underwater video. It's very difficult to manage your legs in the water or to even understand what they're doing. We live on land and we rely on the blunt messages from feet hitting ground to let us know if and how well we're walking or running. There's no reason to think that your brain can accurately track your leg movements when the ground isn't there anymore. We have to teach our legs how to appreciate the nuances of kicking in water in order to eliminate drag, and then to transmit power from our hips. This isn't easy, but Barbie and Ken can help.

Their knees didn't used to bend, but apparently now they bend a little. So can yours. We've talked about kicking in other emails, so use Barbie and Ken to get your kick under control so you know your stress level is down. That's all we care about now. A gentle kick from the hips with your feet pointing toward where you've been.

But you're still sinking. Of course you are. We've only worked out your kick. You want to calm your kick so you can be horizontal in the water. Most people who sink will at this point be about 8-inches below the surface. As long as you're horizontal that's ok for now.

Erin King '08

There are some toys that bind your ankles, and while these little Marquis de Sade devices will eliminate your erratic kick, they'll bring any fears you have in the water to a fine anxiety-attack level as you sink with your ankles clamped together. Don't use them. But as long as we're talking about anxiety attacks, you'll need to appreciate two issues. First, depending on ego and a few physical characteristics, your

Erica Triebenbach '10

head weighs about 10 pounds. As a percentage of your body weight, this can border on insignificant—but just as in real estate, the determining factor is location. Your head is at the end of your swimming body, so anything it does dramatically affects your water position. If you raise your head, the movement will leverage your hips and legs downward. If you lower your head, your hips will pop up, but you'll be introducing drag at the bow of your body. You want your head to be in-line with the rest of your body. You can visualize a rope coming out of the top of your head, pulling you down the pool. When this happens, the natural position of your head will be in-line with your body. You will be looking at the bottom of the pool. If you can't visualize a rope coming out of the top of your head, you were correct if you started this exercise at your feet, because the answer to relaxing in the water from the head-end means asking your brain to work with you. This is the second issue.

Water isn't our home. We have to learn to be comfortable in water before we can swim efficiently. All your drills are designed to help you become comfortable in the water, to reduce your stress. But the interesting point about stress is that often focusing on it makes it worse, so I don't talk a lot about how a drill can reduce stress, I

Mike Noel '07

just watch for the goofy kicking to go away.

In order to reduce stress in the water, you have to deal with your fears—such as not being able to breathe and out-swimming the sea monsters. These are both real fears. And if you don't think they are, ask yourself why you have that goofy kick then?

You want your heart rate to be steady when you first get in the water. This tells you that you are relaxed. Your heart rate shouldn't go up until you get into your aerobic range.

Stop thinking about sinking and start thinking about stroke count. Long, slow strokes will calm you and help you slide through the water. Be aware of your rotation. There are drills where your belly button will be facing the wall—usually some form of a hand lead drill. If you are prone to sinking, doing this drill will be like asking a dog to dance—it might happen but it won't be pretty. When you rotate this way there is very little surface area to keep you afloat. Your drill is stone skipper, which keeps your shoulders at the top of the water and your pecs flat—unlike a hand- or head-lead drill—and allows you to test the buoyancy of your body through gentle pressing on your pecs to generate forward motion. If you don't know what stone skipper is, go to the Total Immersion web site and see the video. http://www.totalimmersion.net

You will realize that coming to the party with a sinking personality gives you the opportunity to learn a few things very right while your less depth-challenged teammates will slide sloppily by. You'll need to achieve balance and relaxation in order to stay somewhere close to the surface—good for breathing. Your teammates will need the same discipline in order to swim better than average—good for winning. I've seen many swimmers who blast by the sinkers in September and then draft off them in November. My money's on a dedicated sinker over a cocky newbie floater any day.

Keeping your shoulders at the surface does not mean becoming the team barge as you flatten out and plow through the water shoulder first. It means you get to learn all about body torque before the floaters do, and you'll learn it because it's the difference between breathing air and growing gills. Keeping your shoulders high keeps your head close to the water for breathing, but if you don't torque your body, you'll lose all the benefits of core power generation. So while you'll keep your shoulders flat, you'll rotate your hips. The twist is in your middle back. Keeping your shoulders high is easier if you keep your elbows high, too. High when you're taking your stroke and high during recovery. This particular move—high elbows, high shoulders, and a torqued mid-section—is difficult because you have to learn it all at once. Floaters have the luxury of learning it at their leisure. You get to experience the magic of the steep learning curve.

Nick Vandam '09

What else do you have to do to achieve a high water mark? Anchor your hand. The angle of your arm is more critical than it otherwise might be. You'll need to find the proper anchor angle for you so you can leverage it to contribute to buoyancy, while placing it at the correct angle to achieve an efficient set-up and catch, which will recruit your lats and abs as you propel your body over your high elbow and shoulder.

Yes, you get to propel your body over your shoulder and elbow. You don't take a stroke pushing your hand backwards. Again, the floaters will do this too, if they ever figure it out. You have to do it. Your prize is that this is the zen secret to fast swimming—body past shoulder—and you thought it just helped you stay on top of the water.

The last point: You'll never float totally on top of the water—and you don't want to. Stay just below the surface. Submarines move more efficiently through the water than boats—V-hull or barges. Enjoy this natural tendency. Just be sure to keep your body sufficiently high in the water so that all you have to do is roll to air. The floaters are likely to do a little corkscrew dance as they twist their head and neck up to air. Watch their hips drop while you get a good catch. Motor by them as their hips drop and they struggle to regain balance.

It's not productive to assume the role of sinker, and it isn't accurate to assume that a wetsuit is your answer to alleviating your bottom-feeding tendencies. Sinking is like any other technique issue.—it's fixable with good coaching, relaxation, and attention to body management. It highlights stroke deficiencies and provides immediate feedback when they're fixed. I think a so-called sinker with a desire to swim well has greater potential than a floater who thinks swimming is easy.

Nick Vandam '09

Practice

Friday, 8 December
50 minutes. Power and Pacing.

Physical: Find your intelligent fast pace and explore movements to increase speed.

Psychological: Stay in control of your stroke. Manage what your body is doing so you remain streamlined and able to generate and transmit power. Break between 100s is to allow you to regain control of stroke count and consistent split time.

Warm-up: 5 minutes. 250 yards. Custom drills if you have them, or 100 hand-lead drill, body facing white board. High hips. Anchored arm at 45-degrees. 100 underswitch. 50 balanced quiet swim. Heart rate <130.

Main set: 40 minutes. 2,000 yds.
- 20x100. 10 seconds rest between each 100. Swim with someone who has a stopwatch. Try to keep stroke count within 3 throughout practice. Keep heart rate less than 150. Try to keep splits consistent with descend for the final 500. Don't start fast. Consistency and sustainability is the objective.
- Keep swimming past 20 repetitions if you can.

Cool down: 5 minutes
- 200 yards. Quiet glide swimming. (25-yd underwater swim to confirm low heart rate is optional.)

Practice

Holiday Break
1–2 hours. Power and Pacing.

Physical: Long easy sets for benchmark splits and stroke count. Speed segments – add strokes, decrease time.

Psychological: Relax. Let the speed come to you. Don't chase a low split.

Warm-up: 15 minutes. Custom drills if you have them or fist swim 100, hand lead with high hips and anchored hand 50, fist swim 100, hand lead 50, long, quiet, slippery swim 200. Repeat for 15 minutes.

Main set: Repeat as often as possible

- 250, 500, 750. Rest is 25, 50 and 75 seconds after the corresponding distance – 25 after the 250 etc. But...stop long enough at every 250 for a comparative time. Count strokes by 250s. Compare strokes. Start slowly. End quickly. Add one stroke/25 on the 750 while holding or descending time. The middle 250 of the 750 is the speed set, but stroke count must stay at +1.
- If your stroke falls apart, drill and then pick up where you left off.
- After each 1500 (250, 500, 750), swim five 100s to learn. Forget the clock, forget stroke count. Learn something about your stroke. Let the knowledge come to you. Relax and be sensitive to swimming. Do something different and note how it affects your stroke. Watch other swimmers while you swim. Analyze their stroke.

Cool down: 10 minutes

- Quiet glide swimming. Low heart rate. Think about swimming. (25-yd underwater swim to confirm low heart rate is optional)

Tracy Wilson '07

Zen Stroke, Beginner's Mind

by Laurie Ferguson, Ph.D.

There's a lot of talk about relaxing in order to swim your best.

But how do you really achieve a state of relaxation when you are getting ready to race? You are excited, nervous and pumped. You need and want that adrenaline—don't you? Being relaxed doesn't seem like part of the picture.

In fact, it seems counter-intuitive. Won't you go more slowly if you are all mellowed out?

Part of the difficulty is in the word and what it connotes.

Relaxed for a sports endeavor is about feeling at ease, at home in your body and in yourself. It does not mean the languorous, half awake feeling you get early in the morning.

In the "racing relaxed" state you are highly alert and very clear minded; you are fully tuned in, not mellowed out. There is no strain. You allow whatever needs to come to your attention to register, but aren't stressing to get information or pacing nervously to distract yourself before you begin. Your body has no jangles; it has a focus and purpose that is laser like yet open.

How do you begin to achieve that mind and body connection?

You start small—and you begin when you are away from the water, from training, from your team and any pressure.

The best beginning is to commit to taking five minutes a day to sit in a comfortable position and do nothing.

That may seem like a nonsense idea, but doing nothing—thinking nothing—is very demanding.

We want to be moving, to be figuring stuff out, to do something mentally or physically.

Some Zen teachers refer to this as "monkey mind"—the mind that jumps everywhere and never stops to land anywhere significant.

But when we never discipline our mind—and part of the discipline is giving it a rest—we are less able to control where it will go.

When you sit still, you are cultivating a relaxed, but attentive mind.

Some people count breaths while they sit. They count four breaths in and eight breaths out.

Some count to ten very slowly and back again. Some just sit and watch their thoughts float by without getting caught by them.

This practice creates some mental space and some ease in your body. You find that over time you have a small oasis of peace. You realize you are not your thoughts and you are not your emotions; you can watch them without being them.

Experiencing this gives you a mental focus that can be relaxed— less grasping at the moment or the emotion. You get some mental resilience.

You can add five minutes at the end of the day to match your five minutes at the beginning of the day.

Or you can go for ten minutes at a time.

The point is that as long as you faithfully practice this simple exercise, you are developing your ability to relax as you swim. Or relax doing anything. You have given your self a new way to swim and a new way to live.

Mental Workout for Relaxing

This workout requires five minutes of private uninterrupted time.

- Sit in a comfortable position. Straighten your spine and plant your feet firmly but lightly on the floor. Let your hands rest on your thighs.

- Hold your head so that your skull sits easily at the top of your neck, and the back of your head is in alignment with your back. Don't let your jaw jut forward pulling your head out ahead of your shoulders.

- Relax your jaw. Relax your neck, your shoulders. Pull them down from your ears.

- Relax your hands, your legs, arms and feet.

- Breathe in slowly to a count that is comfortable for you.

- Breathe out slowly to a count.

- Repeat ten times.

- While you are breathing and counting, let your thoughts float by. Don't follow them anywhere. Stay with your breath and your counting. If you get distracted, gently bring your self back.

- You can focus your eyes on the floor, or on an object like a flower or a picture.

- Let your eyes be very softly focused.

- If you are worried about the time, use a timer for the five minutes. Once you practice this for a week or so, you will intuitively know when the five minutes are up.

- When this begins to be routine for you, and you can feel some of the results, increase your time to ten minutes of breathing once a day.

Welcome to the best relaxation practice known to our world!

Officer in Charge LTC Ralph Vargas and Mike Dason, Nick '07 Dason's father.

Nick Haines '08, swim coach Louis Tharp,
Total Immersion Multisport Director Greg Sautner,
Dave Tyson '07, Tracy Wilson '07, Ashley Morgan '10

Peter Bauleke '10, Nick Vandam '09, Brian Lagasse '10, Nick Dason '07,
Ryan Perkins '09, Rob Sherry '10

Warm-up.
What Is It Good For?

Friday, 5 January

Hi Everyone:

Everybody says warming up is good. It prevents injuries, prepares you to excel, etc. etc., and while nobody is doubting that you should warm up and cool down, it's important to know as much as you can about what is going on during this process.

A warm up is psychological as well as physical. If you know what's happening while you're warming up, you can appreciate it and modify it for maximum benefit.

However, as soon as we think we know the most efficient way to warm up and cool down, somebody does a study and explains what we're doing wrong. It's important to remain open-minded about physical warm up changes, just as you do with changes to the sport itself. We're in this to get better; information is critical. If you want some perspective on how much sport has changed, it

wasn't until the 70s that college football coaches allowed players to drink water during practice. Many of them wouldn't let players drink any liquids until after practice. A coach could get fired for doing that today.

Joe Imbriaco '07

A warm-up has to start slow and it doesn't have to start in the water. Your warm-up could start on the way to the pool. Measured breathing through a slowly quickening pace as you walk will raise your heart rate from resting to about 80. Climbing stairs is good, too. The latest theory is that a slowly rising heart rate pumps blood into the extremities more completely and efficiently than a heart-rate-spike you get from diving in the water and ripping off a quick hundred. Your blood vessels expand, allowing the maximum amount of blood (which carries oxygen) to get to your muscles. This helps ensure efficient energy production by delivering oxygen to the cells and taking away the waste products. This also

allows the connective tissue in your muscles to stretch. (Latest information is that muscles don't stretch, connective tissue does.)

You already know it's not good to stretch cold, so a gradual warm-up allows you to stretch naturally without risking injury.

Gradually raising your heart rate to 140 is a good warm-up.

Andy Stock '10

Psychologically, the warm-up gives you the opportunity to set your practice or race goals. By the time you are ready to race or practice, you should know what you want

Kari Vahle '09, Ryan Peacock '09, Dave Tyson '07

to accomplish and how you're going to do it. So what you do physically and mentally during your warm up will allow you to assess your current state, create realistic goals, and reach them. This is why we have classroom sessions before practice.

Your custom warm-up drills can be divided into fast and slow activities. Start out with the slow ones for the gradual heart-rate increase so you will be able to assess how well your body is responding. If you're doing a hand-lead drill and your hips are lower than you'd like, a short-term goal is to implement the steps to get them higher. If you feel slow, acknowledge it, but don't assume your practice or race will be slow. The two are not connected, especially during

Dave Tyson '07, Tracy Wilson '07

warm-up. Drill through the slowness. Warm-up is not a race. Swim through your drills, check your body position and your mental state, and move into the swim drills (such as high elbow, patient hand, and breathing). Isolate specific areas that need attention and then integrate them back into a complete stroke.

Ask questions. "How do I feel?", "How does this particular drill feel?"—but don't be judgmental. If you feel bad, just note it, don't beat yourself up over it. If you feel great, note this too. While you're doing this you are preparing your body for practice or a race, so any of these early feelings can be wrong. The important part, as always, is to move through the warm-up with respect for your body and your feelings so you can enjoy your race or practice. Ignore other swimmers. Focus inward. Listen to whatever your body is telling you and continue moving through the warm-up. It's important, psychologically, not to stop in the middle of a warm-up. You want to create continuity among muscles and mind. You want to create a smooth flow of energy between your body and your mind. You want to enjoy the confidence that comes from exercising control in a sport that asks you to react decisively to out-of-control situations.

Dave Tyson '07

Your mood during warm-up will help determine your mood during practice. It's important to understand that you have control over your mood. You can decide how you will approach your practice or race. There isn't one right way, but there are fundamental components you can incorporate into your practice personality.

Clearing your head is critical. Your focus needs to be on you, your swimming, your body management, and your practice or race goals. Anger equals injury so get rid of it. A certain amount of anxiety during warm-up (if it is focused on practice or the race) is normal. As COL Sullivan says, "If you have confidence in your training, you will be able to control pre-race or pre-workout anxiety." Whether you are swimming with ease or difficulty during your warm-up isn't important. Having the confidence to accept either as reality and work within your abilities is all that matters. Remembering that you have to look beyond negative feelings is part of having confidence that you will do well regardless of how you feel. And, it's not just about working with negative feelings during warm-up. Positive feelings can give you a false sense of your ability, causing you to exceed your race or practice strategy envelope and get fatigued or go anaerobic when sufficient oxygen doesn't get to your muscles.

Warm-up is about critical thinking regarding your stroke. Speed up for a few strokes. Note how easy or hard it is and then check through each component of your stroke to find out what can be improved. Your stroke is constantly changing; sometimes this is good and sometimes it isn't. When you discover something that will make you more efficient or deliver more power, you will need to imprint this in your neuromuscular system. Acknowledging it and then moving on isn't enough. Your brain and body need more than that in order to add your discovery to your stroke. Replicate it and examine what's happening. Get to know it. Welcome this new improvement the way you would welcome a new person into your circle of friends. When you let your brain and body know you are looking for improvements—and that you will value any improvement—it will occur. It is possible to learn something new every time you get in the water if you create the environment that welcomes change and improvement.

Erica Triebenbach '10

Sometimes you'll want to write about it in your training log. Even if you never read it again, the act of writ-

Nick Vandam '09, Ryan Peacock '09, Tracy Wilson '07, Nick Dason '07, Nick Haines '08, Joe Imbriaco '07

ing it down helps create the permanence you need.

We've talked about letting speed come to you, and warm-up is where you can work on this principle. When you create room for speed, it will be there. Chasing speed doesn't work, especially in a warm-up. Relax into your stroke so your brain and body can become perceptive and sensitive, able to make conscious and unconscious changes, and operate as a cohesive force.

When is warm-up over? About halfway through your practice. How do you know if you have warmed-up properly? You'll be energized halfway through your practice. You'll be ready to go faster. You'll be confident. Your heart rate will be consistent at the rate you choose.

Warm-up is a whole-body and focused-mind activity. If you warm up properly, you will have a descending-time practice. This means your final set will be faster than your first. It doesn't mean you won't work hard. It means you will embrace the challenge, not chase it. It means you will induce stress in order to reach new pro-

ficiency levels and not feel defeated because you didn't go faster. It means you'll be able to manage your body and mind in the water. It means you've created a productive learning environment.

And, it means you'll get to cool-down.

I spent time at the U.S. Olympic Training Center a few years ago swimming in the flume. At regular intervals, the coach would squeeze my ear lobe to get a few drops of

Nick Dason '07 back, Nick Vandam '09 blood from a hole she had made

earlier. The blood
went into a lactic
acid meter, and it
was easy to see
how efficiently I
was metabolizing
this waste prod-
uct of energy
production. The
learning experi-
ence came at the

*Joe Imbriaco '07 and mom, Lynn,
one of the photographers for this book.*

end of the set when she casually said, "Ok, cool down." Cooling
down in the flume means the people in charge have to turn down
the water flow or you wind up nailed to the screen at the back, so
after they did I swam quietly for a minute or so and said, "Ok, I'm
ready for the next set." She squeezed out a drop of blood and
showed me the lactic acid meter. None had dissipated. I thought
my cool down was complete, but it hadn't yet started. There are
ongoing arguments about whether lactic acid that isn't metabo-
lized quickly is harmful. It can stay in your body for up to 24
hours after a hard practice, but a proper cool-down decreases it
dramatically. Less lactic acid is supposed to make you less sore
then next day but...the discussion continues.

Regardless of the role lactic acid plays in your body after practice,
many people don't cool down for psychological reasons. Taking
the time to cool down means inviting thoughts about how awful
they did in practice. How they can't go fast. How they let their
lane mate beat them again. It's a self-preservation tactic—don't
cool down and you don't allow space to think about these things.
Point is that a good warm-up ensures a good cool-down. When
you do the warm-up right, the cool-down is your opportunity to
recap your success while you're lowering your heart rate and gently stretching your muscle connective tissue. Cool-down takes
away the pressure of practice. Often, your swimming is more con-

fident and more relaxed. Check your cool-down time for a 50. It's not uncommon to be cooling down at a near practice pace without feeling stressed. This is an important realization. Work out the Boolean logic: If I can swim at near-practice pace without feeling tired during a cool down, then I should be able to bring this same mental and physical state to my practice in order to become a faster swimmer. Else, I'm not taking advantage of this learning experience.

I've seen swimmers cool down—lowering their heart rate—while swimming at their practice pace. How did this happen? I told them it was a cool down. They relaxed. This is how powerful your mind is. This is why you warm up and cool down—so you can enjoy this power and learn how to use it. This is how you get faster. This is how you let the speed come to you.

Standing: Nick Haines '08, Erin King '08, Ryan Peacock '09, Nick Dason '07, Nick Vandam '09, Rob Sherry '10, Bryan Lagasse '10, Dave Tyson '07, Andy Wassel '08, John Leatherman '08, Ryan Hulst '08, Peter Bauleke '10, Andy Stock '10, Mike Noel '07, Erica Triebenbach '10, Joe Imbriaco '07, Ashley Morgan '10, swim coach Louis Tharp, Emily Sfeir '09, Cristin Browne '09, Head Coach COL Pat Sullivan, Officer in Charge LTC Ralph Vargas. Seated: Nicholas Sterghos '09, Kari Vahle '09, Christine Kawoczka '08, Matthew Vargas, Andy Cahoy '10, Mike Herndon '07, Tracy Wilson '07

Practice

Friday, 5 January
50 minutes, Power and Pacing.

Physical: Consistency. Build speed through power and gliding.

Psychological: Relax. Let the speed come to you.

Warm-up: 5 minutes. Custom drills if you have them, or fist swim 100, hand lead with high hips and anchored hand 50, fist swim 100, hand lead 50, long, quiet, slippery swim 200. Repeat for 15 minutes.

Main set: 1,600 yards 40 minutes
- 100, 200, 300, 400, 300, 200, 100 at a comfortable pace. Start slowly. Begin adding speed on the last 300. Heart rate <160 at finish. 30 seconds rest between each or until heart rate is <130 whichever takes longer.

Cool down: 5 minutes
- Quiet glide swimming. Low heart rate. Think about swimming. Stretch for maximum glide. (25-yd underwater swim to confirm low heart rate is optional.)

Nick Dason '07, Nicholas Sterghos '09, Nick Vandam '09

Peter Bauleke '10, Nick Vandam '09, Nick Dason '07

Bryan Lagasse '10, Nick Vandam '09, Nick Dason '07,
Ryan Peacock '09, Peter Bauleke '10

Congratulations

Tuesday, 9 January

> *Tryouts are held twice a year for the tri team. The first is in August at the West Point Triathlon and the second in in January at the beginning of the Spring semester. This email went to the new team members who made the team in January. This group has a tough challenge. They must quickly catch up to the rest of the team, while they rest of the team continues to move forward. There is always competition between fundamental and advanced mechanics – how much of each to teach in order to create a unified team that swims together.*

Hi Everyone:

Congratulations and welcome to the team. I'm the swim coach for the tri team. I met some of you during tryouts, and I'm looking forward to meeting the rest of you Tuesday.

My immediate objective is for you to get integrated with the team and familiar with practices as quickly as possible. We focus on technique. I assume you all are aerobically fit, and I assume you are motivated to swim 100 percent—so the only way to get better is to improve your technique. And that's my longer-term objective—to give you the tools to swim more efficiently.

Our practices emphasize reducing resistance, generating power from the core and power delivery to your legs and arms. Drills are customized for each swimmer. Practices are periodized so you are able to increase your efficiency in stages, while monitoring your heart rate so that you define your maximum speed at a low (<110 within 30 seconds after finishing) heart rate. Our swim race strat-

egy is to finish with a low heart rate, very little lactic acid build-up, minimum glycogen usage, and in the top third of the pack—but not usually top five, unless we are training for a sprint distance tri, or you are a very gifted swimmer. We can talk more about our training and racing philosophy tomorrow. Within the next few weeks, I will videotape you above and underwater and you will take a 1500-yard efficiency assessment for performance benchmarks.

I've seen your tryout results and I'm impressed. It's clear that some of you have a swimming history. I'd like you to take a minute and send me a brief email about it—pool and open water—if possible before Tuesday's (16 January) practice. If you have been a competitive pool swimmer, let me know which events.

Mike Noel '07

I'm looking forward to getting to know you all, understanding your swimming objectives and incorporating them into our team goals so you can swim faster and more efficiently.

I swim at Crandall Monday and Wednesday evenings (starting 17 January) and I'm happy to lead OYO practices. I'm a Total Immersion coach and work closely with Total Immersion founder Terry Laughlin on team training. You can learn more about me at:

http://www.tgihealthworks.com/about_mgmt_lt.shtml

http://www.tgihealthworks.com/gay/

http://www.overachieversdiary.com/ref.cgi?3

Practice

Friday, 12 January
50 minutes. Drills and Power.

Physical: Getting to know your new friend, the Stone Skipper drill.

Psychological: Let your mind and body get used to this new drill.

Warm-up: 10 minutes. Custom drills if you know them, and stone skipper—at least 100 yards. Yes, I know it's difficult, but it will get easier. 100 yards of gliding/swimming. Very low stroke count.

Main set:
- 200 at a comfortable pace. Stroke count/25. If your stroke count spread was within 3, go to practice (1) below. If it was greater than three then go to practice (2) below.
- (1) 200 apply power and add 1-2 strokes/25. Stroke spread no more than 4. If more than 4, go back to 200 at a comfortable pace and try 200 with power again. Move to 3x200 below when you can do this successfully.
- (2) 100 at a comfortable pace. Stroke spread within 3. Continue 100s until stroke count is within 3, then go to 200 at comfortable pace, 200 with power and +1+2 strokes per 25. Move to 3x200 below if you can do this successfully.
- 5x200 with power (10 secs rest). Stroke count +1+2/per 25. If stroke count goes up, go back to comfortable swim. Stop to leave time for cool down.

Cool down: 5 minutes
- 50 stone skipper. Quiet glide swimming, very low stroke count. Low heart rate. Think about swimming. Stretch for

maximum glide. (25-yd underwater swim to confirm low
heart rate is optional)

Erin King '08

Nicholas Sterghos '09

Glide and Power

Wednesday, 17 January

Hi Everyone:

Last night gave new team members a chance to focus on glide and others to continue to explore power generation as well as glide.

The psychological aspect of the practice, whether you were focused on glide, power or both, was to appreciate the consistency that comes from a disciplined and relaxed approach to conscious stroke mechanics competence. Or, thinking about what you're doing in the water and observing the result.

The physical aspect of the practice was exploring different sensory and muscular issues regarding stroke mechanics and then integrating them. Luckily, most of this happens unconsciously, so for you task-oriented team members, relax. It happened. Stroke counts dropped, kicks settled down, quiet swimming occurred. Life in the water was good.

Power Generation:

We're going to concentrate on maximizing consistency and sustainability in a 250 for the next few weeks. The objective is to bring consistency to stroke count while sustaining your 50-yard split time. This is difficult. The assessment results showed that a lot of people started off too quickly, peaked, and then slogged through the sets. Power genera-

Nick Vandam '09

tion comes from managing your body and your mind. You all are lucky because you are in great physical condition, so you can allocate your attention to being smart and proficient. The smart part comes from understanding that every practice is an exercise in descending times. You must be more efficient at the end of the practice than at the beginning. Anybody can be fast at the beginning of a practice. Smart swimmers understand their energy reserves, stroke proficiency and emotional state, monitor them through the race (or practice) and protect them from early depletion. The temptation to go fast early is strong. Fighting it takes too much energy. Eliminate it as an option.

Your friend stone skipper is busy burrowing into your neuromuscular system while you're busy with the mechanics. How will you know when it's working to help generate power? It's like the day you realized what an intransitive verb is—all of a sudden it made perfect sense—a verb that has a subject but not an object.

OK, maybe you were absent that day. Swim is an intransitive verb. "She swims." Play is a transitive verb. "She plays guitar." "Guitar" is the object. "Swim" has no object. Who knew grammar could help you swim better? Anyway, integrating stone skipper into your stroke will just happen and all of a sudden you'll feel a burst of free speed as you reach to anchor your hand. OK. Forget intransitive verbs. Think of the guy in the TV commercial who smacks his head and says, "I coulda had a V-8™." It'll be that kind of revelation. OK, forget the V-8 commercial, just do the drill. Your overachieving brains will figure it out and surprise you.

Glide:

But this this burst of free speed won't happen if there is no glide—without glide, free speed doesn't exist.

Bryan Lagasse '10 center, after the men's team took third place at the '07 Collegiate Nationals. Only five points separated the top three men's teams.

Practice

Friday, 19 January
50 minutes. Drills and Power.

Physical: See if you can stabilize your stroke count.

Psychological: Relax and think about consistency.

Warm-up: 10 minutes. Custom drills if you know them, and stone skipper—at least 100 yards. Should be easier this week. 100 yards of gliding/swimming. Very low stroke count.

Main set:
- 250 at a comfortable pace. Count strokes/25. If your stroke count spread was within 3, go to practice (1) below. If it was greater than 3, then go to practice (2) below.
- (1) 250 apply power and add 1-2 strokes/25. Stroke spread no more than 4. If more than four go back to 250 at a comfortable pace and then try 250 with power again. Move to 3x250 below when you can do this successfully.
- (2) 150 at a comfortable pace. Stroke spread within 3. Continue 150s until stroke count is within 3, then go to 250 at comfortable pace and 250 with power and +1+2 strokes per 25. Move to 3x250 below if you can do this successfully.

- 5x250 with power (10 secs rest). Stroke count +1+2/per 25. If stroke count goes up, go back to comfortable swim. Stop to leave time for cool down. Don't worry if you don't finish this.

Nick Vandam '09

Cool down: 5 minutes
- 50 stone skipper. Quiet glide swimming, very low stroke count. Low heart rate. Think about incorporating stone skipper into your stroke. Stretch for maximum glide. (25-yd underwater swim to confirm low heart rate is optional)

Mike Noel '07

Erin King '08, Erica Triebenbach '10, Christine Kawoczka '08, Tracy Wilson '07

Dark Water Swimming

Wednesday, January 24

Hi Everyone:

Tuesday night was the blackout practice. The objective was to uncover inconsistent stroke count issues, determine whether your stroke is symmetrical (can you swim in a straight line) and to become familiar with simulated blackwater swimming.

John Morgan talked about focus and positioned it in relation to his life as a blind swimmer where a loss of focus results in injury. He was successful last night if he allowed you to re-draw perspective. Fear isn't getting tangled in weeds, it's hitting a boat propeller. All fear, however, produces adrenaline—and John tries to channel it into swimming focus instead of panic. He said several times that he uses the adrenaline produced by fear—when the sucker fish got on his stomach in Argentina or when mythical sharks chase him in the water—to swim better.

When we talk about stroke count being critical, it's easy to look at it as something conceptual—to attempt consistency, but within a parameter that allows muscling through, regardless of consistency when it comes time to race. Because John, without sight, doesn't have the luxury of short-sighted thinking that slights consistent swimming in favor of cowboy swimming. He is proof that stroke count discipline produces a preferable paradigm of low-heart-rate and predictable results, rather than physical and mental adherence to the old parameter of unpredictable results, high stroke counts, and high heart rates. We practice to race. We don't practice one way and then race another. Everything we do in practice—except for flip turns—is what we do in a race. We practice consistency and sustainability, and we race consistency and sustainability.

The ultimate beauty in a consistent stroke count is the concomitant sustained splits. If you're swimming a consistent 16 strokes per 25 yards, your speed will not vary much. Why is this important? Because it takes less energy to sustain speed than to reach it. If your stroke count is inconsistent, your speed changes with every stroke. You slow down and then you apply power to speed up. Besides producing sloppy swimming and using too much energy, you aren't positioned to improve. Practices become an exercise in slogging. When your swimming is controlled—regardless of speed—you are in a position to assess it and improve. There is a point where improvement will depend on greater aerobic capacity; but long before this threshold is reached, improvement will be determined by your ability to find a controlled, stable pace from which you can grow through the application of proper technique.

Stretch your ankles and, before Tuesday, thank COL Sullivan for fixing the pace clock because after you see Tuesday's practice, your appreciation quotient may diminish.

Andy Cahoy '10, knee brace, injured for Spring Break training in Florida, carried his folding chair around, took pictures and tried to keep from going insane as he watched the rest of the team train all day and race on two weekends. Six months earlier, Andy competed in the New York City Marathon and beat Lance Armstrong. It's true, Lance is a biker, but Andy's a triathlete.

Speed Practice

Tuesday, 30 January

This is a traditional synchronized practice which keeps the team together regardless of lane pace. This allows swimmers to examine the edge of their speed in an organized way, because each segment is on a faster interval. Regardless of which distance/pace you choose, you will begin each segment with the rest of the team.

2800 yards
100 on 2:00 (2:00 pace)
200 on 3 (1:30)
300 on 4 (1:20)
400 on 5 (1:15)
500 on 6 (1:12)
600 on 7 (1:10)
700 on 8 (1:08.5)

2525 yards
100 on 2:00 (2:00 pace)
175 on 3 (1:43)
250 on 4 (1:36)
350 on 5 (1:26)
450 on 6 (1:20)
550 on 7 (1:16)
650 on 8 (1:14)

You never want to take a picture of people eating. This is why.

2525-B yards
100 on 2:00 (2:00 pace)
150 on 3 (2:00)
225 on 4 (1:47)
300 on 5 (1:40)
375 on 6 (1:36)
450 on 7 (1:33)
550 on 8 (1:27)

2150 yards
50 on 2:00 (4:00 pace)
100 on 3 (3:00 pace)
200 on 4 (2:00 pace)
300 on 5 (1:40 pace)
400 on 6 (1:30 pace)
500 on 7 (1:23 pace)
600 on 8 (1:20 pace)

2050 yards
75 on 2:00 (4:00 pace)
150 on 3 (3:00 pace)
225 on 4 (2:00 pace)
300 on 5 (1:49 pace)
375 on 6 (1:42 pace)
425 on 7 (1:38 pace)
500 on 8 (1:36 pace)

1825 yards
100 on 2:00 (2:00 pace)
150 on 3 (2:00)
200 on 4 (2:00)
250 on 5 (2:00)
300 on 6 (2:00)
375 on 7 (1:52)
450 on 8 (1:47)

Nick Vandam '09

1650 yards
  50 on 2:00 (4:00 pace)
  100 on 3 (3:00 pace)
  200 on 4 (2:00 pace)
  250 on 5 (2:00 pace)
  300 on 6 (2:00 pace)
  350 on 7 (2:00 pace)
  400 on 8 (2:00 pace)

Kari Vahle '09

Practice

Friday, 16 February
50 minutes. Drills for Power.

Physical: Stabilize your stroke count while applying power.

Psychological: Relax and think about consistency.

Warm-up: 10 minutes. Custom drills if you know them, and stone skipper—at least 50 yards. Should be easier this week. 100 yards of gliding/swimming. Very low stroke count. Everything is bilateral breathing.

Main set:
- 500. Feel better on the last 25 than the first. Retain lots of reserve. Think about being efficient and enjoy the positive feedback. Anchor, stretch, gentle kick, high elbow, incorporate stone skipper.
- 2x250. Progressively faster. 10 secs rest.
- 500. Progressively faster. Hold stroke count from 250s.
- 2x250. Progressively faster. 10 secs rest.
- 500 (or 750 if you have time). Progressively faster. Hold stroke count from 250s.

Cool down: 5 minutes
- 50 stone skipper. 50 Under hand. Quiet glide, very low stroke count. Low heart rate. Incorporate stone skipper into your stroke. Stretch for maximum glide. (25-yd underwater swim to confirm low heart rate is optional.)

Mike Noel '07

Fear

by Laurie Ferguson, Ph.D.

You approach the water and it's not the pool you're used to—it's a lake. The surface is opaque and you know there will be weeds catching at your feet—who knows what else. You begin to feel the fear in your gut, and suddenly you dread diving in.

There are lots of reasons you can feel fear when you are competing. The swimmers next to you look powerful and you are afraid you're going to get beat, you see the unknown water and images flash of fish nibbling your feet at a critical moment or you remember the last meet and how you flubbed the turn.

When we see or hear something that seems dangerous or even just unknown, the nerve impulses go straight to the medulla—a part of the brain at the base of the skull. The medulla connects to the RAS—reticular activating system. Someone has called this the reptile brain. That's a fairly dismissive description of a part of our mental apparatus that has kept us safe from predators for thousands of years. The RAS connects to our limbic system, the center that sculpts our emotions out of neuro-impulses. Neuroscience says we feel our fear before we realize we are thinking about it. That makes sense because research suggests when the limbic system gets those danger signals it operates 80,000 times faster than the cerebral cortex – the seat of our rational thinking. We have a greased lightning path to generate a feeling of fear.

The RAS doesn't think—it gives the same intense response whether there is a bobcat in your bedroom or a snippy email from a boss. Watch out! Flee! Your hands ice up, your stomach flips—all before your thinking brain has a minute to process what is going on and how you want to respond.

This might suggest that you are a prisoner of your brain chemistry.

Our systems evolved to protect us—to help us escape and survive. That's why they are so powerful and so fast.

But there are some ways to get your cerebral lobes back in the action and hopefully running the show.

Don't start with trying to think or reason. Your body has slipped into survival mode with all your adrenals pouring out action chemicals.

The first line of defense against fear—if you determine there really is no reason to be physically afraid—is to stop and breathe.

Several deep full breaths.

The next step is one you have worked on long before you got to this swim meet.

You have made a plan, you've prepared for the unexpected, so that your mind has been trained to switch to an automatic train of thought.

This only works if you have thought about it - before your RAS took over—and you have practiced your mental plan so often your brain doesn't have to go to the frontal lobes and think through a response, it can switch to a memory chain and pull one out.

So the second step is to be prepared. Make a plan.

What can be part of your plan?

1. Reminding yourself to breathe.

2. Stay in the present. Look around right where you are. Get grounded in the moment. Reassure yourself that you are all right and nothing is harming you.

3. Notice your fear. It is not you—it is a fear of something specific but as yet unreal.

4. Keep breathing.

5. Ask yourself questions about the fear. Stupid questions are great—What's the worst that can happen?, So what if I'm afraid? and so on.

In your preparation, imagine some of the things that scare you—the darkness of the water, the weeds, the feeling of the unknown, powerful competitors. See them in your mind's eye and walk yourself through how you deal with those things. What do you tell yourself? How have you dealt with challenges like this before?

6. Reconnect with Your Best Coping Victories. Remind yourself that you have dealt with scary things before and succeeded.

7. See yourself push on through. Our fear makes us want to flee or freeze. When our hands are shaking and our heart rate is up, we want to stop before we begin. Tell yourself that you can use these physical reactions to move more quickly and be stronger.

We are hardwired to feel fear instantly, but the reality is that most of what we fear is in our heads, not in our environment. Preparation and crafting a plan that you practice is your best defense.

As Roosevelt said, "the only thing we have to fear is fear itself." And that we can prepare to conquer.

Mental Workout for Fear

Today we are working on the fear response. We are going to create your plan for dealing with fear. After we design it, practice it every day for a week.

Think of something or someone who scares you. Get a good picture. Start to feel afraid.

1. Take three deep breaths.

2. Look around you—see what's there in the present. Feel your legs grounded on the earth.

3. Breathe.

4. Reassure yourself that you're okay. Nothing is hurting you at the moment.

5. See your fear as something other then a part of you. Make it a color or an image – preferably a humorous image. One client of mine saw her fear as a big furry groundhog. Imagine just laughing and seeing it run away.

6. Breathe.

7. Remember a time when you were afraid. How did it feel to conquer the fear? What did you do to get past it? What are your best strategies? Think of those in bold letters or pictures. See yourself thriving.

8. Watch yourself push on through and do the thing that scares you.

9. Keep breathing.

Now practice that sequence three times.

Tomorrow practice it again until the images and the breathing are automatic.

Speed. It's All About Speed.

Saturday, 7 April

Hi Everyone:

Today's practice was good for two reasons. You got to tweak your stroke in very specific ways before Nationals, and you are all strong enough swimmers now so that if you're confused or uncomfortable with what we did, you can go back to your existing stroke.

If you decide not to use the new hip body torque, don't worry, when we tear your stroke apart next fall you'll have a lot of time to get used to maximizing the power generation of your core. (Firsties get to keep their existing stroke.)

Use what works. This week is all about giving you an edge that you didn't have when you walked into practice.

One more point for anyone who is concerned or confused about what we did today—sleep on it. Allow your brain to process it. In this particular case it is possible to sleep your way to proficiency. (Actual results may vary. Check with your somnambulist before beginning. Does not apply to finals.)

Here's what we did:

In a series of 50s, 75s and 100s, we built on focal points you already knew.

Emily Sfeir '09

Bryan Lagasse '10

1. High elbow and deliberate drive through the mail slot into the water so your arm is stretched out in front of you at a 40-degree angle and your fingers are pointing toward the bottom of the pool. No low elbows—your arm is stretched out as far as it will go.

2. Patient hand. Once your arm is stretched out in front of you at an angle with fingers pointing toward the bottom, stretch farther. Stretch so you feel it through your lats and down to your hips. This gives you greater length in the water—so you will take advantage of the natural speed of a long boat—and it allows your hand to patiently wait for your stroke to begin.

3. High elbow and high shoulder as you set up for a maximum catch. This means Peter can give up his patented three-inch push-down to grab some water. (A lot of swimmers at Alabama would kill to have his stroke, and wouldn't notice the push-down. I'd give it five minutes on tuscaloosa.craigslist.org before somebody snapped it up. They can have it next year.)

4. Pulling straight back using your forearm and hand (and for Nicholas Sterghos, your upper arm and armpit) to catch the maximum amount of water for a strong stroke. The catch is critical for the power delivery from your core. The catch is the only part of swimming where we want maximum resistance. In every other part of the stroke we strive to attain the path of least resistance.

Christine Kawoczka '08

We want to move through the water as quietly and unobtrusively as possible. But for the stroke, we want maximum water resistance on the hand and forearm. We want to catch as much water as possible in order to move efficiently and quickly through it. Your brain wants your hand and forearm to find the path of least resistance (hence the "S" stroke which everyone thought was cool for about 15 minutes in Olympic swim -time years), and if you let it, your hand will scull around, your arm will turn sideways and you won't find maximum resistance. You have to remind your arm to take the path of most resistance. Remind it a lot. This means a high elbow and high shoulder with your bicep nearly parallel with the surface of the water, but still under the water. We're playing with live ammo here. If you find the path of maximum resistance with a low elbow and low shoulder (see John Leatherman's former stroke), you will eat your supraspinatus. This tiny rotator cuff muscle that keeps your shoulder from falling off will have to accept a huge amount of stress. It won't be happy. How will you know if you're abusing it? You'll be one of those people with ice on your shoulder after practice (not you Erin, yours is different) and a lot of pain when you reach for something in the back seat of your car while driving. Don't go there. I'd rather see you stick with an inefficient power delivery system (the "S" stroke) than maxing out with bad form, pain and the resulting intimate relationship with an orthopedic surgeon, an operating room, and a gown that is open in the back.

Mike Noel '07

5. Now the trickier part. We've talked about how swimming is for smart people and smart can mean figuring out how to do the in-water equivalent of patting your head and rubbing your stomach (or is it the other way around?). This whole swimming thing is about making every muscle in your body work together. This explains why there are so many bad swimmers. It's not easy. The good news is nobody on this team is a bad swimmer. Everyone has improved dramatically this season—so stop for a minute and thank your body and brain for getting you this far. I said stop.

When you are in the anchor position, rotate your hips a little bit farther so you can stretch farther and transmit a jolt of energy through your abs and lats to the tips of your fingers (that are angled downward waiting patiently to work with your forearm to get a great catch). This also reduces your stroke count (as Tracy can attest). While you're at it, ask Rob how easy it is to keep your hips high if you're head is not. He can show you how to do it—both ways—and how easy breathing is when you put the top of your head in the water first.

However, just because you've rotated your hips doesn't mean you need to rotate your upper body to the same degree. If you can keep your shoulders flatter while you rotate your hips, you will generate torque (twist) in your abs and lats. When you take your stroke, you will unwind your hips and this torque will become the kinetic energy torque wants to be. You will be generating power and delivering it to your arms. Now your abs and lats, rhomboids and traps—the big muscles—will be supplying power to your comparatively spindly arms (Dave

Tyson not included), which will do what they do best—transmit this power to the water with maximum catch, and launch your body forward. The tricky part is letting it happen. The only counter-intuitive part of this is maximum resistance during the catch. Just like golf, baseball and roller blading, your hips, abs, lats and traps want to be part of the process. Once you let you brain know they can play, they will.

6. Oh yea, one more piece. The kick. It fits so well into this you'd think our feet were made for kicking. We've talked about a gentle kick for triathlon swimming because the alternative was a glycogen-sapping, lactate-producing, resistance-inducing activity that would have resulted in a broken femur if you did it on land. So your alert coaching staff wisely advised going gentle. But that was November and nobody is on crutches (since Andy threw his out a week ago). Today we worked on a purposeful, deliberate kick that punctuated the hip movement. The great part about rotating the hips and creating torque is that the power can be transmitted two ways—up the body and down the legs. Same energy, two outlets. And

Nick Vandam '09

just as a great look has a lot to do with lighting, a great kick has a lot to do with timing. Today, we worked on getting the timing right so the energy bump from your hips is utilized in your kick.

Let your brain synthesize this. You'll be swimming and all of a sudden you'll feel a surge and then it will disappear. Let the learning come to you. Don't chase it. When it happens, respect it. Don't get frustrated when it temporarily goes away.

The steps are simple, the results are magic. And magic isn't something your conscious mind can control. Cristin nearly figured all this out on Thursday without consciously going through steps 1-

6. All she knew was that she was swimming 1:24 hundreds (while talking). Brian was swimming 1:10s. Peter was swimming 1:07s. Joe was smiling which means he was either swimming fast or just realized that he doesn't have to be CIC anymore. The VanDasons got in three plus sets. Who knows how fast they were going.

The greatest part of swimming is the surprise of improvement. The drills aren't linear. Drill A doesn't necessarily produce proficiency B. Drills are the fuel for improvement. All you need to do is pay attention and hang on as muscle, nervous system, and motivation catalyze into champion.

Dave Tyson '07

Why in the World Are You Doing This?

by Laurie Ferguson, Ph.D.

Motivation is a complicated topic and there are lots of ways to understand it. Some psychologists have defined motivation as the combination of commitment and persistence. Both qualities contribute to an understanding of motivation.

But the most important aspect of being motivated is understanding and becoming clear about your personal, entirely unique "Top Five Reasons Why I Compete in Triathlons."

Take out some paper and write down all the reasons why you train, do drills, sweat, swim, run, and bike.

There are probably lots of them. I hope there are lots of them.

Having multiple pushes and pulls to get you moving is part of what keeps you moving.

Now look at what you wrote. The research divides motivations into two categories: inner (intrinsic) and outer (extrinsic). You probably have both.

Extrinsic motivations have to do with external reasons for doing it.

- I want to win the race.
- I want to look fit so I can attract a date.
- My friends are doing it and I like to be with them.
- I'm trying to get on a particular team. I have to because I am required to participate in some sport.

Intrinsic or inner reasons have to do with your own private concerns.

- I love to swim/bike/run.
- I want to feel fit.
- I like the high of competition; it helps me stay sharp.
- I don't want to have... diabetes, high cholesterol, etc. You fill in the blank.

The literature suggests that a mix of both kinds of motivation is best for staying competitive. But there is a little twist. Intrinsic motivation is the real winner for maintaining both commitment and perseverance.

When you are training and competing for your own inner reasons, defeat, weather, exhaustion or negative feedback will not pull you off task.

So go deeper inside and find out why you want to be doing this.

- What about this sport fuels your passion?
- How does this sport keep you on your toes—and make you happy?

If you don't have those reasons rooted deep in your heart and mind, you may find it difficult to stay with it.

The other twist is a little more surprising.

If you are receiving a lot of external reinforcement for your work—those extrinsic rewards may be undermining your intrinsic (natural and easy) enthusiasms.

They found this when young athletes who enjoyed excelling at their sport got scholarships. Suddenly these young people began to complain that the fun had gone out of the game. They became bored with training and were less motivated to win.

Playing for scholarship money and being expected to win put a different kind of motivational pressure on them. It began to undermine the personal love of the sport that had driven them to achieve first place.

So while it seems that getting rewarded would make someone's commitment even stronger, the opposite effect—a lessening of commitment—is more probable.

Lots of things are motivating, and having a mix of motivators makes it more compelling for you to get out there and play.

But finding some important personal reasons to be a triathlete make it more likely that you will continue to race, long after you've received your medals.

Consulting Coach, Stefan Bill, left, as a member of the Swiss Army, and right, as a USMS All American, multiple medal holder in U.S. and international meets, including national meets in his home country of Switzerland, as well as Germany and Austria. That camo pic haircut wouldn't last an hour at West Point.

Mental Workout for Motivation

- Clarifying your personal and particular motivations for being a triathlete gives you a built-in edge. You know who you are and you know why you're doing what you're doing.

- Write down why you are training.

- Write down what you want to get out of the training and the competitions.

- Go over your list and add whatever else you missed – you want to get every reason you can think of down in front of you. There are no bad or poor reasons. Whatever is meaningful to you is what matters. Be sure that these are your reasons, not your son's or your coach's or your partner's or your teammate's.

- Identify what on your list is an inner motivation – leading to some kind of personal satisfaction, and what is an external motivator – leading to some public recognition or reward.

- If you only have one kind of motivator, whether it's internal or external, see if you can think of at least one reason to compete from the other column.

- Now focus on your internal reasons. These comprise your own Purpose for swimming, running and biking. Maybe it's to prove to yourself that you can do it. Maybe you want to raise awareness of this great sport. Maybe you want to better your own time. Whatever these reasons, they are your bedrock, your foundation for inspiring you on during good times and bad.

- Take both your internal and external reasons and make them into a legible list.

- Keep this list with you in your wallet on your mirror or inside your locker. Refer to it, read it daily and revise it when a new reason emerges.

- Your motivation is your purpose and it is your fire. Tend it.

Where Are Your Toys Henry Ford?

Friday, 8 June

Hi Everyone:

It's summer and it's time to find some toys for these couple weeks before you're back training. But before we talk about the toys you can, and those you should not, use in the pool, I came across a typically short-sighted, misspelled Henry Ford quote. He said, "We want to live in the present, and the only history that is worth a tinker's dam (sic) is the history we make today."

The thought was there, the action was there, but the elegance and accuracy was absent. That was Ford—hard-edged in a time in America's history when that particular personality trait was rewarded. He wouldn't have done well in a study group.

The quote, however, gains elegance when it's applied to what you all did in Tuscaloosa April 21—"the history we make today." But unlike Henry's severely limited view of the world, his place in it, and its reaction to him, West Point is one of the few examples of the successful incorporation of history into the present. Ignoring history at West Point is not an option.

Total Immersion Multisport Director Greg Sautner, Rob Sherry '10

Mike Noel '07

History will be respected and it will be made—and recorded—at West Point, just as it was at the Collegiate Nationals. Keep this sense of history and your contribution to it. Throw away the swimming toys.

Actually, you can keep a few toys—but probably not the ones you like. If a swimming toy allows you to swim faster when you use it and slower when you don't, throw it away. I'm usually a pretty easy-going coach, but not with toys that produce a false sense of speed. This includes 99 percent of them, including beloved pull buoys, fins, and paddles.

Toys are aquatic crack. Here's what happens to your brain on toys: it's happy. Here's what happens to your brain when the toys go away: it's sad. You want to swim sad?

The pull buoy. A great invention that keeps your hips high in the water so you don't have to. Too bad we can't use pull buoys in a race. You're responsible for your own hips while racing. But it gets worse. Because you've conditioned your brain to not have to worry about high hips, the two largest muscle groups—quads and glutes—fall into their maximum resistance position, dragging along behind you when there's no pull buoy. Have fun with that— especially when you try to sight. You'll raise your head and your hips and quads will drop even more. A few more degrees of drop and you would water walk.

But wait, you're saying you can just kick faster and that'll raise your hips and glutes; also, your wet suit has a floatation quotient that acts just like a pull buoy anyway, so why not use the pool buoy in practice? Both are true statements. You could also not stroke with your arms, and kick even faster in order to make up for it. And, you could limit yourself to events where the water temperature is below 70-degrees so you'd always be able to wear your wet suit. These are talk radio arguments—they sound good at the time, but ultimately they just make you stupid. You don't want to introduce any inefficiency into your stroke that you then have to compensate for by recruiting the two largest muscle groups in your body—legs and glutes.

But there's more. What else happens when you use a pull buoy? You disconnect your hips from your upper body. Your hips and legs just follow along for the ride while your arms do all the work. We work all year to generate power from your hips and abs, and transmit it to your arms and legs, and now you want to disconnect that? Not in my water you don't.

Now let's talk about the psychological damage caused by this innocuous piece of foam. First, there's the aerobic disruption when you need it the most—when you're starting to get tired and your stroke is starting to fall apart. Nobody ever uses a pull buoy at the beginning of practice. They wait until they are getting sloppy. They wait until the moment when they need to marshal their physical and mental powers to hold the stroke together, and instead, insert the pull buoy. This is not what you want to be teaching your neuromuscular system. But it gets worse.

Mike Noel '07

Bryan Lagasse '10

What happens when you don't have the plastic crack? You feel slow and sad. How's this for an awful thought. You're in the middle of a race, your stroke is getting sloppy, your heart rate is going up, and instead of moving into the planned phase of the race where you pull your stroke together, lower your heart rate and regain your pace, you spend time thinking how wonderful it would be if you only had your pull buoy. Of all the toys, the pull buoy is the most harmful in the water. However, on a pool deck it is a passable head rest if you want to lie down.

Fins. OK. Fins are not the pull buoy's evil twin. They're not aquatic crack, more like aquatic Percocet. They can be helpful for short periods, but addiction is quick and withdrawal is painful. First, the short story about why they are good—and it is a short story. If they are used for specific people doing specific drills, very slowly, they can help make the drill successful—produce the position and feeling necessary to understand why the drill is important. They are good for any drill requiring gentle forward movement through kicking when otherwise you wouldn't move forward. But I really don't even like them in this instance. If you can't propel yourself with a gentle kick in order to do a drill, there is something wrong. Using fins doesn't fix the problem—it just masks it. Fix your gentle kick first, then learn the drill.

But this is all irrelevant because people who use fins use them for speed—and we're back to feeling good with them on and feeling sad when when they're off. But it gets worse, as it always does with swimming toys. The kick is not where a triathlete gets speed in the water. Speed comes from the core. The legs and arms are the power delivery mechanisms, not the power generation system.

A gentle kick keeps your heart rate and lactic acid low and uses much less glycogen. Tri swimming is not an efficient use of legs compared with running and biking. When your swim is finished your legs should be eager to go to work. Some swimmers will use a rapid and efficient kick at the start of the race to gain early position, and especially in cold water, at the end of the race to get blood flow to them.

But, of course, there's more. Using fins encourages a continuous kick, and tri swimming is more of a two-beat kick. So you're not replicating the race environment.

Unable to justify full-size fins, some people will get the short fins and somehow rationalize that they are better. They aren't. Save your money for a good wet suit.

Paddles. The orthopedic surgeon's friend. The most common upper body technique issue is low elbows above and below the water. A high elbow above the water— as you are beginning to insert your hand in the water—allows you to bring momentum to the reach, maximize your

Erin King '08

Ashley Morgan '10, Cristin Browne '09, Tracy Wilson '07

length in the water, and to find a solid anchor point with your patient outstretched hand. A high elbow while you are taking your stroke provides maximum resistance from your hand and forearm for a huge catch of water, and most importantly, allows you to recruit your hips, lats, abs, biceps and delts for power. A low elbow during the stroke puts all the stress on the tiny four muscles known as the rotator cuff group—and they don't like it.

When you use paddles, chances are good you'll max out the stress on your shoulders because of low elbows. This causes sore shoulders after swimming, and this is never good. If the paddle people cared, they'd put a list of orthopedic surgeons in with every pair of paddles. It's amazing that a simple step ladder has eight warnings, but paddles have none.

But there's more. Suppose you have high elbows. Do you scull? If you do (and most people do) paddles encourage you to find the easy way through the water unless you are very attentive. And, when it comes to stroke, you want to find the most difficult way through the water. Except for the top swimmers, this is high elbow and straight back—no sculling. Try it. It is very difficult because the resistance of the water wants you to scull around it. When team member Dave Tyson realized this, his 100 yard practice time dropped from 1:30 to 1:20. But he's a smart guy; he graduated first in his class.

But, of course, there's more. We're back to the psychological issues of paddles. Once you figure out how to go fast with them, well, unfortunately they aren't allowed in a race. So, as you're racing and thinking about how nice it would be to have paddles, you're not helping yourself do well.

Kick board. It has two good uses. The first is a holder for practices. Wet the paper and stick it to the kick board. Prop the kick board against the starting block. The second is as a balance test. Stand on it in the water. You'll see how the smallest movement can undermine balance. It's a good thought to keep while you're swimming, but it doesn't always translate well from drill to swim. Using it as a kick board to improve swimming is like running behind a car to improve gas mileage. You feel like you've accomplished something, but the two just aren't connected.

The kick board does what all the other toys do—it disconnects your stroke. But there's more. It forces you to raise your head, which means your hips and quads drop, which means you have to kick harder to move forward. You can't rotate in the water and generate power from your core. Instead, you are flat and generate power from your quads and hips while your arms hold on to the board. It's like playing tennis with boots on. I'd say that among all the toys, the kick board is the worst—but I already said that about the pull buoy. At least the kick board has two acceptable uses.

Peter Bauleke '10

The good toys. Yep, there are good toys out there. The definition of a good toy is that it makes you feel better when you stop using it and it forces you to incorporate every part of your stroke into the drill. This encourages integrated swimming and smart body management in the water. Usually, good toys also force you to slow down in order to appreciate what's happening and imprint the right stuff into your neuromuscular system.

Fist gloves or fist swimming. Fist gloves help in three ways. First, they don't allow you to rely on your hand as the propulsive force in your stroke. Second, they force you to stroke with high elbows. Third, they allow you to discover how much surface area can be recruited on your forearm to enhance your catch. The key to practicing with fist gloves—or fist swimming without gloves—is to retain your efficient whole-body swimming technique and count your strokes. The goal is to match your stroke count with and without fist swimming. The difference will be that fist swimming will be slower. When you go back to full hand swimming you should hold the same stroke count, but go much more quickly. This happens because fist swimming requires you to maximize your forearm catch and create power in your core and then transmit it to your arms and legs. It also requires that you maximize your streamlined position in the water in order to minimize resist-

ance. Fist swimming allows you to become a thinking swimmer, not a muscle swimmer. It allows you to become intimate with the water and your place in it. It allows you to get connected intellectually, neuromuscularly, and emotionally. It allows you to set attainable goals and have fun reaching them in a single practice. And, it nearly

Bryan Lagasse '10, Emily Sfeir '09,
Nicholas Sterghos '09, Nick Vandam '09

Dave Tyson '07

free, and takes up virtually no space in your swim bag.

Tempo Trainer. This falls under the category of "whatever doesn't make you crazy will make you a better swimmer." Depending on your interpretation, the beeps from a Tempo Trainer can either result in much better race pacing or much higher levels of free-floating anger. It is a great toy because it gives you continuous feedback, allowing you to pace like a pro. There are two settings: per stroke and per length or set. Start out with the single beep per stroke that helps you create a perfectly timed stroke. Everyone who has used it in this setting immediately says it takes the pressure off of stroke mechanics. It tells you when to stroke. Your patient hand remains stretched out, you prepare your core to generate power and transmit it to your arm, your body glides with minimal resistance, your gentle kick prepares for a two-beat sequence, and then it beeps and you take your stroke—the stroke you have just set up for, the stroke you have just prepared your muscles and your mind to take.

Now move to the three beep setting and every time you flip at the wall it beeps. If you're early or late, you can fix your pace. It is the cruise control of swimming, except unlike the one on your SUV, this one teaches you how to control your own cruising.

But there's more. Tri swimming is about consistency, and that means pacing. The only way to swim faster is to swim fast—smart—increase your

Nick Dason '07

consistent pace. Speeding up and slowing down doesn't help for a whole variety of reasons that we can discuss later. In order to swim a triathlete's 1000 meter race in 15 minutes, you need to swim each 50 yards in 45-seconds. The only way to improve is to swim each 50 yards in 44 seconds. Why? Because tri swimming isn't about finishing first with a burst of speed at the end, or speeding up and slowing down during the race. This uses too much glycogen that you're going to need for the bike and run. The only way to swim a tri is to sustain a consistent pace—and the only way to swim faster is to sustain a faster consistent pace. This is what a Tempo Trainer does—just before it drives you crazy.

Tossing around a flying disc. Rob Sherry '10, Total Immersion Multisport Director Greg Sautner, Andy Wassel '08, Ryan Peacock '09, Joe Imbriaco '07

Stretch cord. Don't think I'm going to reverse my thinking and say it's ok to muscle your way through the water using a stretch cord. That's the easy way to misuse it. The smart way to use it is to swim out until you stop and then try to find a more efficient way through the water so that you begin to move forward again. When you reach your limit using the stretch cord you have the opportunity to work out how to swim more efficiently as well as powerfully. It's the time to use your brain and let your body figure out how to manage under maximum stress. Pick a mark on the wall or the bottom of the pool so you can measure your progress. You will go farther each time if you allow your body and your brain to work together and if you have a good understanding of technique. When you go back to swimming, you and your body will remember how you swam under stress and—when you're under stress in a race or practice—remember how you calmly worked out how to move through the water more efficiently and powerfully.

The worst toy of all, (and I know I already said the pull buoy and the kick board are the worst), is the one which allows you to ignore history. Maybe Henry Ford can ignore history, but you can't ignore your swim history. The idea is to work with history. Improvement is incremental. You are swimming as fast as you can right now. Accept this and work with it. Appreciate small improvements. Good toys help you swim faster if you learn from them.

I haven't covered all the good or all the bad swimming toys. It's important that you are able to rationally decide whether toys help or hurt. The easiest way to determine if a toy is good is that it doesn't give you false speed, efficiency or buoyancy. Your speed, efficiency, buoyancy and body management should improve after you've used the toy. If you want something to make you swim fast, tie yourself to the back of a speedboat. But if you want to be a better swimmer where it counts, when you're racing and making history, use the smart toys that help you get there, not the dumb ones that leave you feeling empty.

Ashley Morgan '10. As a 2007 Plebe (freshman), she was first in Age Group Nationals in Portland, Ore., and third in her age group at '07 Worlds in Hamburg.

Section 2: Math

If you want to measure your speed and efficiency against a larger universe of triathletes, as well as the West Point Cadets, and also keep a real-time record of your improvements, go online at http://www.overachieversdiary.com/. Take the Army Tri Assessment. Easy instructions will show you how to enter your splits and your stroke count for three different sets, as well as some other information in order to get your personal results, and a comparison with others who have taken it.

Swim Assessment 1
21 November & 5 December
U.S. Army Tri Team

Final Results with Written Opinion

Prepared
14 December

The first assessment:
Sustainability and Consistency

About This Document

This document is supported with a personal written opinion. It supercedes the draft documents distributed 5 and 7 December.

This document is a benchmark, a learning tool and a goal creator. At this point in training you are competing against yourself. You are swimming as fast as you can. The only way to get faster is to practice consistency and sustainability. This comes from total focus on technique—gliding, balance and power generation/delivery. Speed will come to you once these objectives are satisfied.

This document should allow you to "touch" your times. It should give you a clear sense of what you can do to improve your swimming and how to do it. If it doesn't, we should talk.

Email me with any questions or corrections.

A note about heart rate: Although we planned to take heart rate readings after each set, most people waited too long to get a reading or didn't get a correct reading. When I looked at the heart rate data, it wasn't usable, so I have not been able to incorporate it into the assessment results. It is listed, but most readings are inaccurate.

Perspective

This is the first assessment. It can be taken as often as you wish. Some people took the assessment twice. In each case the second assessment showed improvement. In order to give you continual goal data, the assessment can be taken as often as you like at practice or on your own with another person to record splits and stroke count. An assessment data collection sheet is included in this document.

A second assessment with the same measurement criteria will be given in January. The difference will be set order. The second assessment will be swum as a 250, 500, 750. This is more difficult than the first assessment, which was swum as a 750, 500, 250. The difficulty increases in the second assessment because the longer set at the end requires sustainability and consistency focus when you are more likely to be tired. The second assessment will also include heart rate monitoring. Your ending heart rate will be a factor in your efficiency rating.

Your goal in both assessments is to move the maximum distance per stroke possible.

A third assessment will incorporate speed (split times) into distance per stroke and heart rate.

In order to be ready for the third assessment, your technique—gliding, balance and power generation/delivery must be at a high proficiency level. In order to help you reach this level, we will focus on creating custom swimming drills at various heart rates that meet your needs. Your commitment will be to understand how these drills contribute to your goal and to conscientiously practice at scheduled workout and on-your-own swims.

Each cadet got a personalized version of the graphs, tables, and charts that follow. They could take the assessment as often as they liked, but most took it twice during the season—Fall and Spring. We measured speed and efficiency and gave them a goal to work towards.

The data on the following pages belongs to a cadet, but we've removed the name and other identifying information.

In addition to this quantitative data, I wrote each cadet a personal opinion of the assessment, and a custom drill list. The personal opinions are not included to protect cadet privacy.

Main Graph

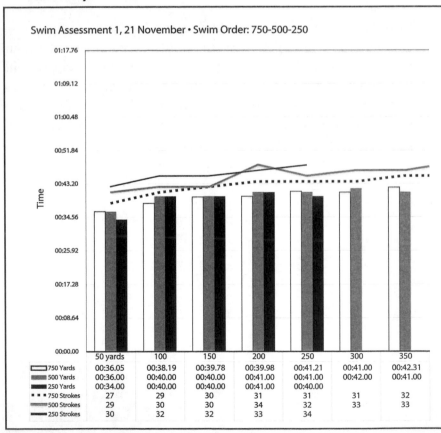

Swim Assessment 1, 21 November • Swim Order: 750-500-250

	50 yards	100	150	200	250	300	350
750 Yards	00:36.05	00:38.19	00:39.78	00:39.98	00:41.21	00:41.00	00:42.31
500 Yards	00:36.00	00:40.00	00:40.00	00:41.00	00:41.00	00:42.00	00:41.00
250 Yards	00:34.00	00:40.00	00:40.00	00:41.00	00:40.00		
750 Strokes	27	29	30	31	31	31	32
500 Strokes	29	30	30	34	32	33	33
250 Strokes	30	32	32	33	34		

Contents: Main Graph

The main graph, below, shows your splits (the white, gray, and black vertical bars) and your stroke count (line graph) by 50s. The white bar and dotted line represent the 750, the gray bar and line are for the 500 and the black bar and line are for the 250. The line should be nearly straight and the bars should be close to the same height. This would represent a consistent stroke count and a sustained 50 yard split. You can compare your progress, for example your split and stroke count at the 200 mark in all three sets. It should be the same. The data table at the bottom of the graph has splits and stroke count values, which allows you to do this.

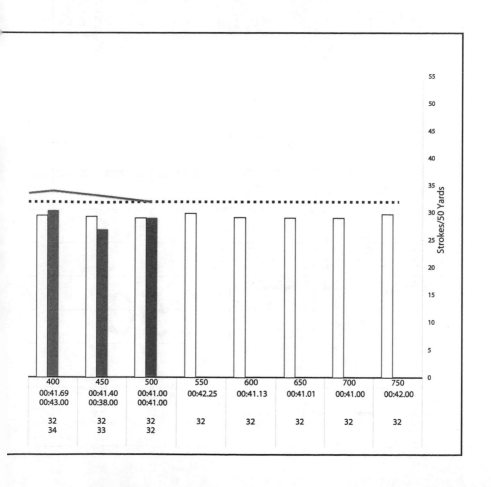

	400	450	500	550	600	650	700	750
	00:41.69	00:41.40	00:41.00	00:42.25	00:41.13	00:41.01	00:41.00	00:42.00
	00:43.00	00:38.00	00:41.00					
	32	32	32	32	32	32	32	32
	34	33	32					

Train Race inspire
West Point Triathlon Team, Swimming Assessment, Part 1, 21 November

Height	Total Mean Strokes	Total Median Strokes	Inches/Stroke	Efficiency Index
73	32	32	56	77%

Speed Index 87.72%   10% Improvement 28 strokes

Summary	Splits (min.sec.00)	Stroke Count/50 yds
Mean	00:40.67	31
Median	00:41.01	32
High	00:42.31	32
Low	00:36.05	27
Max Range	00:06.26	5

750

HR at finish 126
HR 30 seconds 126

Yards	Split		Elapsed Time	Stroke Count Split	Stroke Count
50	00:36.05		00:36.05	13/14	27
100	00:38.19	00:02.14	01:14.24	14/15	29
150	00:39.78	00:01.59	01:54.02	15/15	30
200	00:39.98	00:00.20	02:34.00	16/15	31
250	00:41.21	00:01.23	03:15.21	15/16	31
300	00:41.00	-00:00.21	03:56.21	15/16	31
350	00:42.31	00:01.31	04:38.52	16/16	32
400	00:41.69	-00:00.62	05:20.21	16/16	32
450	00:41.40	-00:00.29	06:01.61	16/16	32
500	00:41.00	-00:00.40	06:42.61	16/16	32
550	00:42.25	00:01.25	07:24.86	16/16	32
600	00:41.13	-00:01.12	08:05.99	16/16	32
650	00:41.01	-00:00.12	08:47.00	16/16	32
700	00:41.00	-00:00.01	09:28.00	16/16	32
750	00:42.00	00:01.00	10:10.00	16/16	32

Summary	Splits (min.sec.00)	Stroke Count/50 yds
Mean	00:40.30	32
Median	00:41.00	32
High	00:43.00	34
Low	00:36.00	29
Max Range	00:07.00	5

500

HR at finish 150
HR 30 seconds 120

Yards	Split		Elapsed Time	Stroke Count Split	Stroke Count
50	00:36.00		00:36.00	14/15	29
100	00:40.00	00:04.00	01:16.00	16/14	30
150	00:40.00	00:00.00	01:56.00	15/15	30
200	00:41.00	00:01.00	02:37.00	16/18	34
250	00:41.00	-00:00.00	03:18.00	16/16	32
300	00:42.00	00:01.00	04:00.00	17/16	33
350	00:41.00	-00:01.00	04:41.00	17/16	33
400	00:43.00	00:02.00	05:24.00	17/17	34
450	00:38.00	-00:05.00	06:02.00	16/17	33
500	00:41.00	00:03.00	06:43.00	16/16	32

Summary	Splits (min.sec.00)	Stroke Count/50 yds
Mean	00:39.00	32
Median	00:40.00	32
High	00:41.00	34
Low	00:34.00	30
Max Range	00:07.00	4

250

HR at finish 130
HR 30 seconds 120

Yards	Split		Elapsed Time	Stroke Count Split	Stroke Count
50	00:34.00		00:34.00	15/15	30
100	00:40.00	00:06.00	01:14.00	16/16	32
150	00:40.00	-00:00.00	01:54.00	16/16	32
200	00:41.00	00:01.00	02:35.00	17/16	33
250	00:40.00	-00:01.00	03:15.00	17/17	34

Contents: Max Range and Data Tables

The tables at left contain your swim data for the 750, 500, and 250 sets. Above the table is your split and stroke range for each set. Both numbers, for range, should be small—less than 5 seconds and fewer than four strokes. It's better if the numbers decreased from one set to the next.

Your name and height is shown at the top. Height is used in several calculations. You will also see your total mean (average) number of strokes, total median (most common stroke count), inches you moved forward per stroke and an efficiency index (which is the percent of your body height covered in each stroke).

The maximum efficiency index any tri-team member had was 134 percent. Your efficiency index can be more than 100 if you exceed your body length for each stroke.

There is also a 10 percent improvement goal cell, which shows how many average strokes per 50 yards you will need to take in order to improve your efficiency index 10 percent.

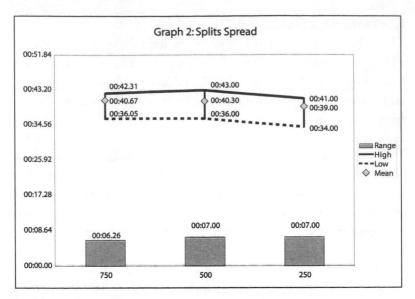

Graph 2: Split Range

Optimally, the boxes on the graph will be short and trending downward. This means the difference between your slowest and fastest splits is very small, and you got faster as the set progressed. The bars at the bottom of the graph show your split range. These bars should trend downward or stay even.

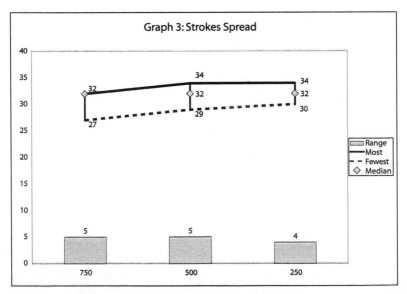

Graph 3: Stroke Range

The boxes should be short and be level or trend slightly upward. The upward trend would indicate a slight increase in stroke count as you near the end of the set and hold or increase your speed. A level box line would indicate a consistent stroke count to the end of the race.

What If...*My stroke count increases?*

The fix is to pay attention to your arm entry. High elbow, and accelerate your arm as it enters the water. Stretch to find your anchor position. Make sure you have a patient hand. Anchor it with fingers pointing downward for at least 1 second. Set up for your stroke by raising the elbow of your leading hand and pushing straight back when your other arm accelerates as it enters the water. Make sure you pay attention to your patient hand. It stays anchored until the entering arm/hand is in the water. This will decrease your stroke count.

What If...*My splits and stroke count are inconsistent?*

This is all about pacing. The first indication when you're swimming will be your stroke count because it's difficult to judge time. So treat this as a stroke count exercise. Follow the directions above and try to bring rhythm into your stroke. Visualize speed skating or cross-country skiing, which will involve your core body. Be aware of bringing your hips into play as you stretch out with a patient hand. Solving inconsistency issues means slowing down on the fastest laps and speeding up on the slowest. Don't be afraid to slow down. When you achieve your pace, the speed will come back to you.

What If...*I'm exhausted after 150 yards?*

When you begin a triathlon, you will not have had the chance to drill or warm up properly. Competitors tend to jump in the water and take off much too quickly. The combination of cold water, no warm-up, and no drill sequences means the probability of going anaerobic in the first 150 yards is great. If you are exhausted after

150 yards, you went into an anaerobic state at the start. The fix is to relax, lower your heart rate by swimming slowly and smoothly, and then find your pace as quickly as possible. The athletes who start out quickly, fade quickly. If you control your start by thinking of the first 200 strokes as your warm-up, you will be able to swim the race aerobically and with a low heart rate. The swimmers who raced at the beginning will come back to you by the one-third mark or sooner.

What If...*My stroke count and times for the different sets aren't consistent?*
If you swam a 1:05 split at the 400 mark of the 500 yard set, and a :55 split at the 400 mark of the 750, this shows fatigue. Pacing early in a race, and attention to streamlining and efficient power delivery, prevents this.

What If...*In order to conserve my energy I slow down at the end of the swim? This keeps my heart rate low for the bike.*
You're talking about not swimming a descending time. The best strategy is to swim a descending time. However, descending times are not achieved at the end of a race. Your strategy is to swim slowly at the beginning to allow for a proper warm-up. By the end of the race you are warmed-up, on pace, and easily able to beat your starting splits without increasing your heart rate. This allows you to swim a descending time. In addition, you cannot swim fast for 90 percent of the race and then slow down for the last 10 percent in order to conserve energy. You will have used more glycogen than necessary for the swim, you probably will have been anaerobic or borderline, and your slow finish may work against you psychologically when the people you passed earlier begin passing you.

Working at the Edge

or

The Goldilocks
Method of Training

by Laurie Ferguson, Ph.D.

Remember the children's story of the three bears? When Goldilocks discovered their house, she found chairs, bowls and beds that were "too big," "too small," and "just right." The principle of the edge is based on that theory—that there is a place "too big" for each of us, "too small," and "just right."

Do you know where your edge is?

Edge is found at the intersection of a level of skill and a level of challenge.

Your edge is where your skill meets a challenge that is "just right"— neither too hard nor too easy.

If you choose a challenge that is too simple, you become bored and may lose interest.

If you deal with challenge that is way beyond your ability, you are likely to become frustrated or discouraged and give up.

When you match your skill with a challenge that is demanding, but not overwhelming, you become more energized and focused and you can usually improve.

Some athletes think about this when they choose a training partner.

If you work out with someone who is much less accomplished, it encourages slacking off. You are less likely to push yourself and much less likely to improve.

Some people like to stay at that comfort level in their training. They work out with others who are at their level or a little below it—and they wonder why they don't swim faster.

There is no edge. Try practicing in a lane next to someone who is slightly better.

You will push yourself to keep up or maybe even surpass them. When you practice that way consistently, you will find you have ramped up your training without too much effort. You have created an edge for yourself that pulls you to expend a little more effort and therefore to believe you can accomplish more.

When you vary your training routine, you can design a different kind of edge. Maybe you are always a solo player. You don't involve yourself much with other athletes. An edge for you might be choosing to help another swimmer or runner. You deliberately workout with someone whose pace is slower because you are offering to inspire and motivate them. Training at that edge can motivate you to perform better because you are teaching.

There are a variety of edge places in training; places where we match our skill with the just-right personal challenge. This is the fastest and most effective way to improve in a sport or in any endeavor in life. Finding your edges is a way to keep your personal learning curve stimulating and fun.

Are You a Mathlete?

Math is always logical. Swimming usually isn't.

If you're a mathlete you probably look at swimming in a time-frame. Sets are a series of numbers. There's something to this per-spective. So for those of you who don't think math when you're wet, we're looking at a new dimension to your swimming.

First, the easy stuff. How do you count a 200? 25, 50, 75, 100, 125, 150, 200? 1, 2, 3, 4, 5, 6, 7? When do you change numbers? At the beginning of the length or when you complete it? Do you count strokes and laps? This is the simple stuff. It's not really math, it's just counting. If this has confused you already, you're not a mathlete. But it's something worth thinking about and codify-ing—especially counting strokes. When your stroke count is off, your stroke is off and so is your speed and efficiency. Stroke count is the early warning. If you can't be a total mathlete, being a count-er can bring big returns. But I think everyone can find a place on the mathlete continuum.

If you know your stroke count for 25 yards, you can convert this to meters (multiply by 1.1). Most tri swims are in meters. Look at the course. Estimate the distance between buoys. Calculate your probable stroke count. Use this as a real-time performance bench-mark.

If you're not a mathlete, you're thinking wind, chop, crowded water, and inaccurate measuring can throw your stroke count off so far that it's useless. Might be. Mathletes don't think so. They use it to understand the effect of these conditions on their stroke, not the other way around. It's just a different way of looking at the world of wet in the middle of a race.

Jim Bolster, the men's swim coach at Columbia, also coaches a Masters tri swim club. He's a mathlete coach. He can explain a practice three different ways, using number patterns. Some swimmers don't get it. They stare up from the pool looking like dogs waiting to be fed, while others are completely connected. One of the interesting side effects of a mathlete coach is the effect these number-structured practices have on your body. A simple every-third 25 as stroke, instead of freestyle, resets your body and allows you to take a fresh look at your freestyle. It's a cranial muscular event that's difficult to explain, but it's a good enough reason to encourage triathletes to learn the three other swim strokes.

Janet Harris is a mathlete. She's an elite Masters swimmer who holds the age group title for the two-mile open water swim. Swimming math provides pure energy during her workouts and her races.

"I'm obsessive about splits," she says. "I need to see every 50. A 1:20 is a good aerobic pace. How much am I under a 1:20 pace? How much under the minute, the 20 or the 40?," she adds, referring to the twenty-second blocks that make up a 1:20 hundred yard swim.

"But," she says, "if you start at the top, it's either vertical or horizontal for a 1:30 pace," she says describing the second hand position on a non-digital pace clock, which she prefers over a digital one.

"You can picture the position," she says of the hands, which she looks for when she flips, which is why she doesn't like the pace clocks with four hands. But, she prefers any clock to another swimmer for pacing.

"Math is what I think about when I'm swimming. If I swim a 200 I try to negative split it. It gives me motivation.

"Open water swimming? There's no clock to look at. I'm not as focused on splits. I'm doing more looking around. There is a sense of freedom. I count strokes. I work hard for 20 strokes."

Math is the strongest rationale for practicing tri swimming in a pool. If you are sensitive to math, you can track your progress and it's the only way to sensibly push your limits. But a lot of swimmers use the pace clock to reinforce what they've already achieved because it's easier to calculate.

But Janet talks easily about calculating the difference in tracking a 1:18 hundred vs. a 1:20. "You are gaining two seconds for each 100, (if you swim a 1:18 vs. a 1:20) so instead of a 6:40 (after each 500), you would be at 6:30—the clock would be vertical for each 500."

She has solutions for all speeds. "The 50 split for a 1:35 hundred is plus 47-plus-seconds. (Plus means it's 47 plus a fraction. In this case 47.5 seconds.) Picture the clock at 35 and 10, then bisect the angle of the second hand for your split. It will show up at the 47 and the 17."

The easiest way to calculate splits, she says, "is to figure out how far it is from the 10s. So a 1:23 to a 2:17—that would be a 1:00 (from 1:20 to 2:20). then minus six seconds—three extra on the front and three less on the second one which makes :54," she says sounding like a savant, but actually only like someone who has found a high comfort level with a calculation that involves base 60 and base 10.

"There is a control and a motivational factor that comes from math. I would prefer to race the clock rather than other people. The clock is always constant. It means I'm very much in control of my workout and my race."

What to do: "Pay attention to splits. Make this a goal. Pay attention to what you come in on. Note your time. Then descend those. Makes practice so much more interesting once you pay attention to what you are doing, then what you are doing for your splits. Then start thinking about negative splitting. Makes things more interesting."

The trouble with topics like this is if you're not already into the subject—already a mathlete, you're probably not still reading. Mathletes will get energy from reading this. The rest have moved on.

But moving on doesn't help. We're going to talk more about the role math plays in improving your speed and efficiency, so if you haven't gotten this far, all this will be news to you when we talk about it at practice. We will find a way to incorporate math into practice, at everyone's comfort level, so that everyone can benefit.

Math may replace stone skipper as your friend, and if it does, you can thank Janet Harris.

Section 3: Motivation

Patterns on Planet Earth Provide Energy for Tuscaloosa

Tuesday, 3 April

I believe in patterns.

It's easy to create a history of verbal assertions that match wishes, but patterns record actions and are the only reliable predictor of future performance.

In two seasons, this team has created an enviable pattern. Galveston proved that you can compete against the best. This was not always true.

More importantly, Galveston proved what the coaching staff has seen all season—your individual development continues to quickly move forward. And because there is a strong sense that the

Kari Vahle '09

power of the group exceeds individual power, this team is overall the strongest and most cohesive in Army tri's short history.

Navy brought a few of its elite in a strategy play that isolated the best to feature individual strength. Army brought 23 to emphasize group power, team cohesion and four years of future strength.

The pattern is clear. We take on challenges as a group and we understand the value of experience and participation. We get it: individual excellence achieved with respect for the team produces unstoppable momentum. Energy is transferrable and increases when it is shared among people with the same goal.

I watched the swim from the mud at the finish—along with a photographer, an EMT and an injured Navy tri team member who wasn't competing. His reaction to the unexpected strong Army finish set off a chain reaction that put Navy on notice. This was not triathlons as usual on planet Navy. This was planet Earth, and Army was strong and deep. As the wet suits came off to reveal Army singlets, he worked in real time to realign his expectations. Two of his remarks were telling. The first was obvious: "Where did these strong swimmers come from?", but the second proved the pattern when he said, "They don't look tired," as several of you smiled and talked to me as you ran through the snot-nosed, high-heart-rate, stumbling competitors who didn't possess your understanding of tri swimming strategy.

The midshipman was young, and at this point intellectually and emotionally disoriented at not seeing his teammates in the lead—or at all—so I let reality, not me, give him the lecture on arrogance in sport.

Bryan Lagasse '10 and half of John Dubiel, a Navy midshipman, who spent a semester with Army as an exchange student. (Although rivalry can run pretty high between Army and Navy, I didn't cut him in half to feed into this. He's a great guy, and there's a full picture of him elsewhere in the book.)

There are many ways to beat an opponent. The most satisfying is to know that you've created the perfect synthesis of training, desire, emotional stability, psychological readiness, and reliance on team. It gives you the ability to win, and it makes your opponents nervous. There is energy in the universe and Navy felt Army energy Sunday through the humid Galveston air.

In order to draw energy for the future, look at patterns. This team identified goals and exceeded them. Everyone is dramatically better today than a few months ago—dramatically better. Take time today to recognize this. Let yourself know you appreciate the work you've done, because I believe no other collegiate tri team has improved as much as Army—certainly not Navy. They came to the season with

Mike Herndon '07

little room for improvement, and this is bad. The incredible part of improvement is that it creates the kind of exponential momentum that other collegiate teams will call an overnight success. Nothing causes competitors to worry more than improvement. It rattles them. It takes away their preconceived notions of predictability. It's what makes sport exciting. It's what creates champions.

And just as we have combed Galveston's results for strategic and tactical advantage at Tuscaloosa, you can be sure Navy—and several other schools—have identified and marked all of you. And ha—probably for the first time. Enjoy it and draw energy from the attention.

The world got Army energy in Galveston. Tuscaloosa will get it next.

What You Get is What You See

by Laurie Ferguson, Ph.D.

Do you have an imaginary pool? A private place where you are fast and sure, confident and relaxed? If you see yourself in that pool, or feel the water and the muscles powering your stroke, then you are on the way to practicing one of the most important skills for a performance athlete.

Most elite athletes report that they use mental imagery to improve their training. They work out their technique, prepare for events, rehearse a new skill and relax in their imagination. Yet as effective as this mental practice is, many athletes don't take the time to figure out how to create a scenario and persist with regular run-throughs.

Nick Dason '07

There is nothing mysterious about using the imagination. Most of us waste the power of our inner theatre by daydreaming or acting out little dramas. To harness your mental power to improve your swimming, biking or running involves choice and discipline.

Start with that inner pool. Dream up and design your pool. Make the water as inviting as possible. The best temperature, the right lighting, and feel to the pool deck – a pool where you want to swim and do your best.

Then create a scene where you are swimming. There are two ways to use imagery – one is by watching yourself,

Rob Sherry '10, Nick Vandam '09, Nick Dason '07

the other is by imagining that you are doing whatever activity you want to learn or improve. Both methods are useful and effective, and each works better for certain things. For instance, if your coach gives you a way to tweak your stroke and you have a hard time getting it, see yourself swimming using that stroke. Watch yourself cut through the water, making it happen. Now switch and be in your body. Go through the stroke in your mind, step by step. Imagine what it will feel like to do it correctly. Practice in your mind a number of times, feeling where the glitches are, the hesitations, the not-quite-there aspect to the movement. Go over this and practice, repeating what you need to do and correcting your errors. You have probably done this before in a casual way when you have gotten absorbed in learning how to do something new. The power and magic of inner imagery happens when you make this mental habit a part of your regular training.

You can use it to calm and psyche yourself before a competition, to deal with a tough training situation and/or to motivate yourself when you are getting bored or tired during a drill. Your imagination is a powerful support for what you are working to achieve. Just choose to use it!

Contributing photographer and Air Force Academy graduate
Patrick Vandam. He's Nick '09 Vandam's brother, Nick Dason '07

Emily Sfeir '09, Rob Sherry '10

Training Confidence

Friday, 13 April

Hi Everyone:

First, thanks for respecting Mickey Wender, the swimming head coach, when he asked for quiet last night at the end of his practice—the beginning of ours—for his team-building exercise. He's a huge and valuable tri-team supporter and we're incredibly fortunate to be using his pool.

Second, Andy Cahoy is back in the pool and the world is a better place.

Last night was swimming tune-up night. The purpose was confidence. The four exercises were a mind-body check for Tuscaloosa. The Tempo Trainer®, stretch cord, three dark swimming and spotting lanes, and the 500-descend lanes were there to make you feel good—because this coming week is really all about you. If you have any doubts that it's all about you: when I say it's ok for Ryan to try to break the stretch cord, and he does, it's clear that it's all about you.

Nicholas Sterghos '09

Confidence, and its recipe for creation within a team, is an interesting concept. In 1969, a young, talented quarterback, Joe Namath, who made a name for himself during high school in Beaver Falls, Pennsylvania, and then at the same place we'll be next week, the University of Alabama, said at a press conference before Super

Joe Imbriaco '07

Bowl III (back when it was easy to read the Roman numerals) that the New York Jets would beat the Baltimore Colts (yes, they were in Baltimore back then). The Colts were 16-1. The Jets weren't. But Namath led the team to a 16-7 victory, holding off the only Colts score until the fourth quarter.

(Before we go any farther, don't assume I'm the only gay man in America who's a font of football trivia. What I know about football comes from being on the road with Joe for five years in another life. I don't know a first down from a hockey goal.)

Joe was at the Miami Touchdown Club dinner and was speaking. Someone from the back started heckling him and he said, "Wait a minute, let's hold on. You Baltimore guys have been talking all week, but I've got news for you, buddy. We're gonna win the game. I guarantee it."

Now before you jump ahead to the place in this story where Joe gets MVP and the Jets make history without Astroturf or the warmth of Miami, there is an important intermezzo.

When Weeb Eubank (the Jets coach at the time) heard Joe's comment, he went nuts. Eubank, besides being from Indiana (along with Nick Haines, Nick Dason and Andy Wassel -- where did all these Hoosiers come from?), was a strategy coach. The Colts and the country assumed the Jets were going to get their cleats handed to them. Eubank was banking on the Colts being more cocky than Namath—which might not have been a reality-based assumption—but it was popular perception. When Namath announced to the world that the Jets would beat the Colts, the media jumped on it. Joe had put the Colts on notice. Joe's teammates felt the pressure. Weeb and Joe had a serious discussion about talking too much, but Joe said, "Coach, I'm just doing what you've taught me to do—be confident."

When we were on the road, a lot of people asked Joe what he would have done if the Jets had lost Super Bowl III. He would say, "I would have showed up for practice the next day." But then he would immediately flash the Namath grin and say, "but I'm glad we won."

Nick Vandam '09

The Jets were more than underdogs at Super Bowl III. They were the best team in a raggedy league that no longer exists. They went into the game with skill, strategy and confidence and came out with Super Bowl rings. The Colts were more than the favorites— they were the best team in the best league. They went into the game with a long history of victory, famous, seasoned players, and a famous coach. But past performance is only a predictor of future success if you're on the sidelines. When you're competing you own opportunity, and opportunity trumps history.

Last night COL Sullivan and I had the chance to step back and watch. We were looking for problems, but we saw confidence.

Practice is almost over. You are the best triathletes you have ever been. And while you can look forward to getting even better if you're on the team next year, it's time to be in the present and own this opportunity. That's how you make history. Otherwise, history is just an anchor.

Nick Dason '07

Ryan Peacock '09

Nick Dason '07

Practice

Thursday, 26 April
50 minutes. Power and Pacing.

Physical: Find your intelligent fast pace and explore movements to increase speed.

Psychological: Stay in control of your stroke. Manage what your body is doing so you remain streamlined and able to generate and transmit power. Break between 100s is to allow you to regain control of stroke count and consistent split time.

Warm-up: 5 minutes. 250 yards. Custom drills if you have them, or 100 hand-lead drill. High hips. Anchored arm. 100 high elbow. 50 balanced quiet swim. Heart rate <130.

Main set: 40 minutes. 2,000 yds.
- 20x100. 10 seconds rest between each 100. Try to keep stroke count within 3 throughout the workout. Keep heart rate less than 150. Try to keep splits consistent with descend for the final 500. Use the pace clock. Don't start fast. Consistency and sustainability is the objective.
- Keep swimming past 20 if you have time.

Cool down: 5 minutes
- 200 yards. Quiet glide swimming. (25-yd underwater swim to confirm low heart rate is optional.)

Nicholas Sterghos '09

What Do You Believe?

by Laurie Ferguson, Ph.D.

> *"I can't believe that," said Alice.*
>
> *"Can't you?" the Queen said in a pitying tone. "Try again; draw a long breath and shut your eyes."*
>
> *Alice laughed. "There's no use trying," she said. "One can't believe impossible things."*
>
> *"I dare say you haven't much practice," said the Queen. "When I was younger, I always did it for half an hour a day. Why sometimes I've believed as many as six impossible things before breakfast."*
>
> *-Lewis Carroll,*
> *Through the Looking Glass*

How many impossible things do you practice believing?

Or, like Alice, are you stuck in a thinking habit you label "being realistic"?

Confidence, that mysterious elixir of attitude and presence, is one part experience and two parts belief.

Strong competitors are always building their confidence by practicing (that's the first element) and by examining and controlling their beliefs (the foundational practice).

Ryan Peacock '09, Peter Bauleke '10

Only with consistent discipline

can you form a bedrock of confident belief in yourself that will sustain you during losses, mistakes and fearful times.

So what are the elements of developing confidence?

Many people assume it is the obvious—winning or being good at something. But studies show that all winners aren't confident, nor does losing dampen confidence—in some people.

It has much more to do with your perceptions of why something occurred—how you frame it to yourself.

Nicholas Sterghos '09

So let's look at your perceptions or beliefs about why something happened.

When you win, what do you say or think about it?

Psychologists tell us that when we believe our success is personal, controllable and customary, we will build our confidence. That means saying to yourself, "I have the ability, I have the competence and I can do it again."

On the other hand, when something negative happens, we build our confidence by believing that the adverse event was impersonal, random and unusual. This means we say to ourselves (and therefore begin to believe), that happened because the weather was lousy, it was a mistake I can correct, and besides it just happened today, and probably won't tomorrow.

Unfortunately, some of us use these beliefs in the wrong order. We believe our successes are ran-

Cristin Browne '09

dom and out of our control and our failures are personal and completely in our control.

We create a script where "luck" and circumstances brought together a victory and our own lack of talent or willpower inevitably decided our defeat.

Maybe that's because you were taught to be modest—not to assume that you are better than anyone else. That kind of belief system won't help you win races.

You don't have to be arrogant—just confident.

Explain that you win because you practice—that's something you control, you are good—that's your personal ability, and you can do it again—it's a part of your makeup.

Explain your losses as something random—not a usual event that you expect. Explain your mistakes as something you can correct, maybe happening because of weather or a bad night's sleep—in

other words because of something momentary and out of your control.

Try this—in your mind explain your last bad practice that way. Do you feel the little bubble of confidence start to expand?

You can create beliefs that will increase your confidence. Believing new things only takes practice.

Mike Herndon '07

Another Speed Workout

Thursday, 3 May

Hi Everyone:

Andy Cahoy and I practiced last Saturday and Andy Wassel and I practiced Monday. Since Andy Cahoy is getting back into the water, we focused on pacing through gliding. And since Andy Wassel is relatively new to swimming, we practiced gliding, too, but we didn't call it that.

Mike Noel '07

Gliding is the gateway to swimming fast. Without it, you cannot transmit core power to your arms and legs. With it, you can not only put power to the water, but you can engage in active rest during a race, control your heart rate, and stay relaxed and flexible.

Gliding is the perpetual motion machine in swimming. It's the free speed you find by preserving previously generated speed. It's the coast. Gliding diminishes the slowing process between strokes. It allows a constant speed to be sustained, and is solely responsible for a consistent low-heart-rate pace.

What upsets glide? Resistance.

What encourages glide? A long streamlined posture in the water. It's that simple—except we're not fish, so it's not that simple. If you watch fish, they glide. They don't swim. They'll use core body strength to transmit power to a tail fin which provides power bursts. After that, it's all about preserving speed. When we talk about fish-like swimming, this is what we mean. Humans have to learn to swim efficiently—fish don't. On the other hand, fish have to learn to like dining hall food, and that comes naturally to cadets, so there is balance in the universe.

One distinct advantage fish have over humans in the water is that they don't have knees. (This is also why fish don't ride bikes.) Knees upset glide in the water. Don't bend them. It is not possible to achieve movement on land without bending your knees, but it is not possible to achieve glide in the water if you do. Bent knees are like brakes. The largest muscles in your body, your quads, become your anchor when they go outside of your body line and disrupt your glide. Once that is finished, your calves do the same thing. Problem is that most swimmers don't know they're bending

their knees. Here's how to find out. Kick on your back. If your knees come out of the water, you're bending them. Let your feet point toward the wall and create a boiling pattern in the water by kicking just below the surface. Think Barbie. She has knees, but they don't bend. I'm not sure about Ken or GI Joe.

Glide is deceptive, however, and it's most deceptive at the beginning of a race. It is important to be able to identify glide vs. fresh power. When you first start, you have fresh power. Life is good. You swim fast. You feel like you could do this all day. This isn't good use of glide—this is bad use of

Andy Stock '10

glycogen. You can't sustain this speed, and your body tells you this at about 300 yards when your muscles tighten, your stroke falls apart, and you slow down.

So how do you know when you're gliding at the beginning of a workout? Stroke count and Tempo Trainer. Neither of these is available in a race, but your brain is, so you need to imprint this information: Never start out fast just because it feels good. You can practice this in the pool using stroke count and Tempo Trainer. Your stroke count should be low and you should be flipping on three beeps. As you hold your pace through the set, you can add a stroke or two in order to get to your usual stroke count.

Andy Stock '10

But it feels so good I must be doing something right. It's difficult to let go of the initial feeling of speed when you go out fast. But here's why you have to let it go. First, you're projecting. You want to feel this good throughout the entire race or practice, so you think starting this way will make it happen. That's like getting ready for retirement by not going to work. It feels great at the beginning, but then there's that paycheck issue. Retirement is the result of working, and sustained speed is the result of glide.

Nicholas Sterghos '09

Second, as good as it feels to go out fast, it feels even better when your competitors start swimming back to you. If you're having trouble with this concept, it's when you pass them. But when you think about passing other swimmers it's too easy to assume that you have to increase your speed. This is not the case. All you have to do is sustain your speed. They are the ones who are paying the price for going out fast and enjoying that initial power rush. You are the one who has paid no price and will enjoy the satisfaction of watching them slow down and swim back to you as you easily overtake them. And, not only have you paid no price in energy, when you pass them, sustaining your original pace, you get to take their energy. Enjoy it. In the swim portion of a triathlon, you want to be passing your opponents without depleting energy stores. This can only happen when you are the consistent swimmer and they are not. The swim portion is not the time to be chasing down opponents. It is the time for sustained speed at a consistent pace. Not all swimmers will come back to you and allow you to easily overtake them and their energy, but that's ok. Your job in the swim is to be fast smart.

Getting fast smart means being consistent. If you are swimming 23 seconds on the Tempo Trainer—a 1:32 hundred—for a 500, the only way to get fast smart is to swim 22 seconds—a 1:28 hundred. It's not productive to swim fast at the beginning and slow at the end, even if this nets a 1:25 average. Why? Because erratic swimming has limits. Your potential for continuous improvement is decreased when your pacing is erratic because you use too much energy. The only way to improve tri swimming times is to achieve consistency and then consistently increase your pace.

Peter Bauleke '10

For the Firsties

Tuesday, 15 May

> *This was my email to the departing seniors, known at West Point as "Firsties."*

Hi Firsties:

This email isn't about glide, power or balance. Or about pacing.

Actually, yes it is. It's just not about swimming.

Last night Joe and I swam together, and as much as I wanted not to, I had to leave his stroke alone—except for a few things, of course—as he prepares for Xterra and Alcatraz. It was difficult not to focus on the potential that signaled even more progress, but there was more than enough glide, power, balance and pacing to carry him through. And I'm not talking only about swimming.

None of you were proficient swimmers when you joined the tri team. All you brought was your athletic talent, commitment, perseverance, positive disposition, and a desire to learn. And that's all you needed. West Point provided the environment that encouraged excellence, and your accomplishments have proven the value of this environment—and of the team. And I'm not talking only about swimming.

Against overwhelming odds of any sort of swimming success, you've all permanently raised the prerequisites to join the tri team. The finishes at Nationals, and the depth of the team's talent, means we can

Peter Bauleke '10,
Ashley Morgan '10,
Emily Sfeir '09 back,
Nick Haines '08,
Joe Imbriaco '07

build on your work. But it's also possible that because of the team's high proficiency you may be the last group of non-swimmers. We may not again see the dramatic improvements you all have made. And this is unfortunate because I was a non-swimmer, too, and know what it feels like to enjoy quantum leaps in proficiency.

Let's talk about those odds against success. Pick your swimming dream team. Here are your choices: a boxer, a football player, a spiritual brainiac, a five-foot-one-inch-body-in-a-six-foot-sport, and Joe (who eludes description). The men have enough muscle mass to sink like a boat anchor, and Tracy barely makes the minimum height requirements for USAT. But Tracy makes it and the men don't sink. You are proof that past results are not the predictor of future performance. And I'm not only talking about swimming.

Last night, while Joe and I were working on a new 25-power/glide drill for next fall, and then while Joe was chasing muscle fatigue—from earlier lifting—against the three beeps of the Tempo Trainer, I wondered if swimming, for all of you, had become a good part of your life.

I wondered if when the dry-land world of power, balance, or pacing got out of control, you'd think about swimming as a way to reconnect, finding a parallel between the gentle persuasion of the water that shows you how to maximize your power, and the same gentle persuasion necessary to maximize a leader's power.

I wondered if when you need emotional or physical rehabilitation, you'd think of how swimming could contribute, and whether you would summon the same enthusiasm necessary for success that was so readily summoned for swim practice—and national ranking.

I wondered if Joe would make his set, but, like the rest of you, he already had. And I'm not only talking about swimming.

Practice

Wednesday, 23 May
Pacing Ladder.

Hey everyone:

I feel terrible. Sore throat. I need to back out of swimming tonight. I've been putting off making a decision about this all day hoping I would feel better, but it hasn't happened.

If you are going to swim and want a workout, try this:

Keep the same stroke count and pace. Ten seconds rest except where noted.

    50
    100
    150
    200
    250
    300
One minute rest
    500
One minute rest
    300
    250
    200
    150
    100
    50

I've attached a spreadsheet so you can put

Mike Herndon '07

in your 100 pace and it will tell you what you need to swim in the other distances in order to remain consistent. Only fill in the cell with the box border. The rest is magic.

'Nick Dason '07, Nick Vandam '09

Swim coach Louis Tharp, Joe Imbriaco '07

Bryan Lagasse '10, Andy Stock '10

Quotes Don't Win Races

Monday, 25 June

To the five cadets chosen to compete in the 2007 Age Group Nationals:

If you go out the back door of the Class of '62 room, there's a dark area you pass through on your way to the new addition or upstairs. High up on the wall, just above where I used to do sit-ups, is that quote from General MacArthur.

Quotes don't win races, and unless they resonate with you, they aren't likely to be remembered. Training and confidence in training wins races. Luck wins races. And of course, determination—just not quitting—wins races.

It's summer and there may not be the usual high energy around to keep you focused, but it's just because of this that you will rely on yourself and each other to create the energy necessary to compete successfully in Portland. The coaching staff has talked among ourselves about discipline vs. self-discipline. We know what you know: coming to coached workouts takes discipline. When nobody's watching, it's self-discipline.

Christine Kawoczka '08

I know you've got workouts, and technique emails, and all the coaches are here if you have questions or comments. You've also got our energy and positive thoughts with you, whether you're visualizing, practicing or racing.

Oh yea, that MacArthur quote: *"On the fields of friendly strife are sown the seeds that on other days and other fields will bear the fruits of victory."*

Five cadets went to the USAT Age Group Nationals in Portland, Oregon. One woman and four men. The woman, Ashley Morgan, brought home the gold in her age group. In their age groups, Cadet Nick Dason finished fourth, Nick Vandam finished 11th, Nicholas Sterghos finished 20th, and Rob Sherry finished 35th. Nick Dason returned from deployment—Iraq—in January and finished in the top five of every tri between then and Nationals. Nick Vandam swims for Army as well and is a consistently high finisher. Nicholas Sterghos competed in his first Triathlon in April. Nationals was his fifth race. He joined the team in January after running track for Army.

Joe Imbriaco '07

What's Your Story?

by Laurie Ferguson, Ph.D.

I imagine you as an athlete who works hard. You concentrate on your drills and get yourself into the water as often as possible. You want to compete at the top of your class.

In every way you are training to be a first class swimmer.

Well, in almost every way.

In your mind you carry on a conversation with yourself and think of yourself as the short clumsy kid you once were. You feel that learning a new stroke technique is an effort, and you always remember how hard it was for you to learn new things. You hear the voice of your first swim instructor, and there's a quick burn of shame as you think about how frightened you were of the water.

Maybe those examples aren't yours, but I bet that you have your own drawer of negative or upsetting scenarios that you consider "your story," an "accurate" description of who you are.

But is it really accurate?

Or merely an old mental routine?

Erin King '08

Old stories often hold the theme of being a victim of circumstance, a loser, or someone who is afraid. They can be comfortable because they help us stay small, excuse what happens to us, and we begin to believe that this is just who we are.

But this is not who we are. It's just a version of our life that we repeat.

Are you ready to give it up?

In order to train at your highest level, you need to change your story.

This can be harder than it sounds.

We've told our version so often we think it's the Truth—some permanent part of our character or our ability.

Yet it is just a story—a particular lens we've chosen to use when we think about ourselves.

Cristin Browne '09

What we're after here isn't creating some fairytale version of yourself—it's more like adjusting the script from Eeyore to MacGyver; from "Nothing ever happens right for me" to "I've made this kind of thing work out before."

Start by describing yourself—no downer descriptions allowed. How would you tell me about yourself?

I recently asked a young man why he was taking such a difficult path. His answer was quick and easy—"I like a challenge."

His story was that transparent.

What's your version of your motivation?

Are you a strong, innovative athlete who meets challenges head on?

A determined, effective swimmer who is always looking for the next learning curve?

Someone who enjoys swimming and has the heart of a dolphin?

Weave stories about yourself using words that give you energy or inspire you. See pictures of yourself in an easy, engaged motion. Then practice that story so it becomes part of you. Weed out any tendencies to blame or whine, diminish or demean. Tell it to your friends, your teammates; write it in your journal.

This is who I am. This is how I got here. This is where I'm going.

A strong, positive back-story is a major source of your power. A dynamic story underlines and strengthens any training that you do. It supports you in difficult or demanding times.

Your best ally for moving forward with power and grace is the story of your life, authored by you.

Joe Imbriaco '07, Swim Coach Louis Tharp

Joe Imbriaco '07, Andy Stock '10, Bryan Lagasse '10

When Does the Mental Process Kick In That Says It Is Ok To Cheat?

Thursday, 26 July

You're training hard, seeing results, living through the positive pain, striving to keep body and mind pulling in the same direction, trying to capitalize on mistakes and setbacks, staying prepared for a lucky break, and keeping your thoughts focused on the pure act of being the best every time you get in the pool. Every

time you get on your bike. Every time you run.

How do the Tour de France riders fit doping into this paradigm? How do they displace integrity? How does a baseball player make cheating an ordinary training partner?

Nothing is ordinary about being part of the U.S. Military Academy triathlon team. Army Tri is extraordinary. It is a gift you create and then accept with humility. The mental and physical training is something we embrace. Our uncommon goal is balancing our true limits, which we don't know, with our ability to reach them, which we ultimately discover. This produces champions. In '07, National Collegiate contenders and age group medalists. We know the unfettered thought process that catalyzes activity, stress and continuous training, cannot survive cheating. It can-

Chris Iten '06, Iraq

not co-exist with purity of thought that is critical to accomplishment.

We know when it co-exists with victory, integrity is lost. The concept of integrity preceding victory—as well as defeat—is what allows us to make sense of the unpredictability of competition.

When integrity doesn't precede victory, nobody grows—not society and not you. We all take a collective step backwards, even if the cheating is never uncovered.

Doping is intellectual and physical dishonesty. It is a high act of self-hatred. It is punishment for the rest of an athlete's life because it requires living with knowledge of the act. It out-Shakespeares Shakespeare. It permanently clouds the pure emotional path to success. How come some riders in the Tour de France and some baseball players don't know this? Were they absent that day? Are they going to apologize when they're tired and beaten 20 years from now? Do they even see the the problem?

When the team suffers loses, when Mr. fast plebe Peter Bauleke's bike falls apart at nationals, he chooses to run alongside teammates who started in a later wave instead of obsessing about his misfortune. When Nick Dason, who took a year off to study abroad—in Iraq—is bleeding and undernourished, he chooses to finish a half-ironman and then redouble his training and share his learning. When we're faced with formidable competitors who seem to have natural advantages, we have faith in our training. Everyone on this team has earned a personal story of integrity and humility that provides individual and collective energy. It's too bad those doping athletes didn't have the same opportunity. Maybe then they'd know that when irrational thoughts replace critical thinking and emotional commitment, fantasizing that cheating is a way to ensure victory becomes the illogical imperative.

Keep training. You'll keep getting better. We all love to win, but your goals are personal and they're not affected by single victories or defeats. Whether you finish first or 138th, be satisfied with your hard work, welcome the chance to work harder, expect continuous growth, and be proud of your contribution to Army Tri. And as you continue to get them, put your medals away and put your integrity on display—not the other way around.

Practice

Thursday, 26 July
38 minutes, 1,900 yards.

Whether you've been training consistently or not so much, this workout will get you in touch with pace and stretch your speed limit.

Warm-up (10 minutes, 400 yards). Custom drills, include stone skipper, patient hand and anchored hand. Be aware of body position and controlled kick.

Pacing Segment:
- 500. Three 25s at pace and sprint one 25. Repeat to 500. Object is to see how quickly you can regain pace and stroke control after the sprint. Measure this by stroke count on the second 25 vs. the fourth. Stroke count on sprint not more than +3.
- 500. Two 25s at pace and sprint two 25s. Same objective: measure stroke count to determine how quickly you regain pace. Stroke count on sprint not more than +3.

Cool down 10 minutes – 500 yards.

- Stay long in the water. This means take fewer strokes. Stroke count for each 25 yards should be three less at the cool down than at the warm up. Pay attention to technique.

When you think you are cooled down, swim one length (25 yards) underwater taking a normal breath at the beginning. You should reach the end of the pool easily, and not be out of breath. If you can't, you aren't sufficiently cooled down. Your heart rate before doing this should be 110 or less.

The Worlds Is Yours

Thursday, 23 August

> *I sent this email to the five cadets chosen to represent Army on Team USA at the Hamburg BG Triathlon World Championship 2007.*

Hi, Ashley, Bryan, Nick, Nicholas, and Nick:

Nick Vandam '09,
Nick Dason '07

For most of your military career, when you leave the U.S. you're likely to be doing the nation's business in a hostile area.

But not when you go to Hamburg for Worlds in a few days. It's what makes Worlds significant. It's not only about you being the best West Point has, and it's not about you meeting personal goals—although these are valid reasons for being selected to go. It's about your opportunity to do the nation's business peacefully and powerfully. When you accepted your place on the team, you put yourself in this bigger picture.

Champions are not created from the top down by coaches or institutions. They grow from the bottom up in a rich environment. You've all acknowledged—many times—the structure at West Point and within the team that has

Nick Vandam '09, Head Coach COL Pat Sullivan,
Nick Dason '07, Bryan Lagasse '10,
Nicholas Sterghos '09, Ashley Morgan '10

propelled you to this elite level, but it is you who have created your champion status. It is you who have been able to piece together the teaching and practicing so you could reach inside and create your personal formula that resulted in your success at Age Group and Collegiate Nationals, and your invitation to Hamburg. You are the alchemists.

I think it's important that you understand how creatively and uniquely you've been able to combine the necessary components to reach this championship level. This understanding is what makes your elite status your own. It is what COL Sullivan means when he asks you to have confidence in your training. It's what LTC Vargas means when he says "good morning" after pulling the trailer 22 hours to Tuscaloosa. Your training is yours and knowing how deep its results go—knowing how far into your conscious and subconscious this training resides—knowing this is where ultimate power lives. It means you can call up this power when you need it.

It means you can accept and process the unknowns in every race with the knowledge that you will create positive energy that will support you. It means that you know—not hope—you can compete with the best. It is the difference between a pure elite competitor who does the nation's business peacefully and powerfully and a Hamburg tourist.

Ashley Morgan '10 and her mother, Donna

Out of the approximately 5,000 competitors at Worlds, the U.S. Army Tri Team finished in top 1 percent in their age group.

In the Olympic Distance event:

- Ashley Morgan '10 took bronze in her age group, 87th overall.

- Nick Dason '07 finished 39th in his age group, 121st overall.

- Nick Vandam '09 finished 49th in his age group, 154th overall.

- Nicholas Sterghos '09 finished 56th in his age group, 209th overall.

In Sprint Distance, Bryan Lagasse '10 finished 30th in his age group and 139th overall.

Head Coach COL Pat Sullivan, Bryan Lagasse '10, Nicholas Sterghos '09, Nick Dason '07, Nick Vandam '09, Ashley Morgan '10

Index

Notes

Notes

Notes

Notes

Notes

Notes

Notes

Notes